50 Low-Calorie Asian Soup Recipes for Home

By: Kelly Johnson

Table of Contents

- Miso Soup with Tofu and Wakame
- Vietnamese Pho with Chicken and Rice Noodles
- Hot and Sour Soup with Shrimp and Vegetables
- Tom Yum Soup with Mushrooms and Lemongrass
- Chinese Egg Drop Soup with Spinach
- Korean Seaweed Soup with Tofu and Shiitake Mushrooms
- Thai Coconut Curry Soup with Vegetables
- Japanese Udon Soup with Bok Choy and Seared Tofu
- Soba Noodle Soup with Miso-Glazed Salmon
- Thai Tom Kha Gai Soup with Chicken and Galangal
- Chinese Wonton Soup with Shrimp and Bok Choy
- Vietnamese Bun Rieu Soup with Crab and Tomatoes
- Korean Kimchi Soup with Tofu and Spinach
- Japanese Clear Soup with Enoki Mushrooms and Daikon Radish
- Thai Tom Yum Goong Soup with Shrimp and Lemongrass
- Chinese Hot Pot Soup with Sliced Beef and Napa Cabbage
- Indonesian Soto Ayam Soup with Chicken and Turmeric
- Vietnamese Canh Chua Soup with Pineapple and Fish
- Japanese Miso Ramen Soup with Shiitake Mushrooms and Spinach
- Thai Spicy Noodle Soup with Shrimp and Rice Noodles
- Chinese Corn Soup with Chicken and Scallions
- Korean Doenjang Jjigae Soup with Tofu and Zucchini
- Japanese Sukiyaki Soup with Thinly Sliced Beef and Noodles
- Vietnamese Bun Bo Hue Soup with Spicy Beef and Rice Noodles
- Thai Green Curry Soup with Chicken and Eggplant
- Chinese Hot and Spicy Soup with Pork and Vegetables
- Korean Tteokguk Soup with Rice Cakes and Beef
- Japanese Tonjiru Soup with Pork and Vegetables
- Thai Tom Yum Talay Soup with Mixed Seafood and Lemongrass
- Chinese Egg Flower Soup with Corn and Chicken
- Vietnamese Bun Mang Vit Soup with Duck and Bamboo Shoots
- Korean Samgyetang Soup with Ginseng and Chicken
- Japanese Ochazuke Soup with Grilled Salmon and Green Tea
- Thai Gaeng Jued Woon Sen Soup with Glass Noodles and Tofu
- Chinese Seafood Congee with Rice and Vegetables

- Korean Sundubu Jjigae Soup with Soft Tofu and Kimchi
- Japanese Chawanmushi Soup with Steamed Egg and Shrimp
- Thai Spicy Lemongrass Soup with Chicken and Rice Noodles
- Chinese Winter Melon Soup with Pork and Shiitake Mushrooms
- Vietnamese Bun Rieu Cua Soup with Crab and Tomato Broth
- Korean Yukgaejang Soup with Spicy Beef and Vegetables
- Japanese Nabeyaki Udon Soup with Tempura and Egg
- Thai Pad Thai Soup with Shrimp and Rice Noodles
- Chinese Chicken Corn Soup with Egg Ribbons and Vegetables
- Korean Janchi Guksu Soup with Hand-Cut Noodles and Beef
- Japanese Oden Soup with Various Fish Cakes and Daikon Radish
- Thai Peanut Noodle Soup with Chicken and Vegetables
- Chinese Clear Vegetable Soup with Tofu and Chinese Greens
- Vietnamese Bun Thang Soup with Chicken, Egg, and Vermicelli
- Korean Kimchi Jjigae Soup with Pork Belly and Tofu

Miso Soup with Tofu and Wakame

Ingredients:

- 4 cups dashi (Japanese soup stock)
- 3 tablespoons miso paste (white or red)
- 1/2 cup tofu, cubed
- 2 tablespoons dried wakame seaweed
- 2 green onions, thinly sliced
- Optional: 1 tablespoon soy sauce
- Optional: 1 tablespoon mirin (Japanese rice wine)
- Optional: Sliced mushrooms, for extra flavor

Instructions:

1. Prepare the Dashi: In a pot, bring the dashi to a gentle simmer over medium heat. If you're using instant dashi powder, follow the package instructions to prepare it.
2. Rehydrate the Wakame: Place the dried wakame seaweed in a bowl of water and let it soak for about 5 minutes, or until it becomes soft and rehydrated. Drain and set aside.
3. Add the Tofu: Once the dashi is simmering, add the cubed tofu to the pot. Let it cook for about 2-3 minutes, or until heated through.
4. Dissolve the Miso Paste: In a small bowl, whisk together the miso paste with a few tablespoons of hot dashi until the miso is fully dissolved and smooth.
5. Combine the Miso Paste: Add the dissolved miso paste to the pot of simmering dashi and tofu. Stir gently to incorporate the miso into the soup.
6. Add the Wakame: Add the rehydrated wakame seaweed to the pot. If you're using any optional ingredients like soy sauce, mirin, or sliced mushrooms, add them now as well.
7. Simmer and Serve: Allow the soup to simmer gently for another 2-3 minutes, being careful not to let it boil (as boiling miso can affect its flavor). Once heated through, remove the pot from the heat.
8. Serve: Ladle the miso soup into serving bowls and garnish with thinly sliced green onions. Serve hot and enjoy!

This Miso Soup with Tofu and Wakame is perfect as a light appetizer or a comforting dish on its own. Adjust the ingredients and seasonings according to your taste preferences, and feel free to customize it with additional vegetables or protein if desired.

Vietnamese Pho with Chicken and Rice Noodles

Ingredients:

For the Broth:

- 8 cups chicken broth (homemade or store-bought)
- 1 onion, halved
- 3-inch piece of ginger, sliced
- 3-4 whole star anise
- 3-4 cloves
- 1 cinnamon stick
- 2-3 cardamom pods
- 1 tablespoon fish sauce
- 1 teaspoon sugar
- Salt, to taste

For the Soup:

- 8 oz rice noodles (banh pho)
- 2 cups cooked chicken breast, shredded or thinly sliced
- 2 green onions, thinly sliced
- Fresh cilantro, chopped
- Bean sprouts
- Thai basil leaves
- Lime wedges
- Sriracha sauce or chili oil, for serving
- Hoisin sauce, for serving

Instructions:

1. Prepare the Broth: In a large pot, add the chicken broth, halved onion, sliced ginger, star anise, cloves, cinnamon stick, and cardamom pods. Bring to a simmer over medium heat. Reduce the heat to low and let the broth simmer gently for about 30-45 minutes to allow the flavors to meld.
2. Cook the Rice Noodles: While the broth is simmering, cook the rice noodles according to the package instructions. Once cooked, drain and set aside.
3. Strain the Broth: After the broth has simmered, strain it through a fine-mesh sieve or cheesecloth to remove the solids. Return the strained broth to the pot.

4. **Season the Broth:** Stir in the fish sauce and sugar into the broth. Taste and adjust the seasoning with salt, if needed.
5. **Assemble the Soup Bowls:** Divide the cooked rice noodles among serving bowls. Top with the cooked chicken breast slices.
6. **Add Garnishes:** Ladle the hot broth over the noodles and chicken in each bowl. Garnish with sliced green onions, chopped cilantro, bean sprouts, and Thai basil leaves.
7. **Serve:** Serve the pho hot, accompanied by lime wedges, Sriracha sauce or chili oil, and hoisin sauce on the side. Let diners customize their bowls according to their taste preferences by adding the desired amount of condiments.
8. **Enjoy:** Enjoy this comforting Vietnamese Pho with Chicken and Rice Noodles as a satisfying meal, packed with delicious flavors and textures!

Feel free to adjust the ingredients and garnishes according to your taste preferences. You can also add other toppings such as thinly sliced onions, jalapeños, or thinly sliced beef if desired.

Hot and Sour Soup with Shrimp and Vegetables

Ingredients:

- 4 cups chicken or vegetable broth
- 8 oz shrimp, peeled and deveined
- 1 cup mixed vegetables (such as sliced mushrooms, bamboo shoots, sliced carrots, and baby corn)
- 3 tablespoons soy sauce
- 2 tablespoons rice vinegar
- 1 tablespoon sesame oil
- 1 tablespoon cornstarch mixed with 2 tablespoons water (slurry)
- 2 eggs, beaten
- 1 teaspoon grated ginger
- 2 cloves garlic, minced
- 2 green onions, thinly sliced
- Salt and pepper, to taste
- Optional: 1 teaspoon chili paste or Sriracha sauce for extra heat
- Optional: Chopped cilantro or parsley for garnish

Instructions:

1. Prepare the Broth: In a large pot, bring the chicken or vegetable broth to a simmer over medium heat.
2. Add Shrimp and Vegetables: Add the shrimp and mixed vegetables to the simmering broth. Cook for about 3-5 minutes, or until the shrimp turn pink and opaque and the vegetables are tender.
3. Season the Soup: Stir in the soy sauce, rice vinegar, sesame oil, grated ginger, minced garlic, and optional chili paste or Sriracha sauce. Taste the soup and adjust the seasoning with salt and pepper as needed.
4. Thicken the Soup: Slowly pour in the cornstarch slurry while stirring the soup continuously. Allow the soup to simmer for another 2-3 minutes, or until it thickens slightly.
5. Add Beaten Eggs: While stirring the soup in a circular motion, slowly pour in the beaten eggs in a thin stream. This will create egg ribbons in the soup. Continue stirring gently for about 1 minute to cook the eggs.
6. Finish and Serve: Remove the soup from heat and stir in the thinly sliced green onions. Taste and adjust the seasoning if needed. Ladle the hot and sour soup into serving bowls and garnish with chopped cilantro or parsley, if desired.
7. Enjoy: Serve the Hot and Sour Soup with Shrimp and Vegetables hot, and enjoy the flavorful combination of savory, tangy, and spicy flavors!

Feel free to customize this soup by adding other vegetables such as sliced bell peppers, snow peas, or water chestnuts. You can also adjust the level of spiciness according to your preference by adding more or less chili paste or Sriracha sauce.

Tom Yum Soup with Mushrooms and Lemongrass

Ingredients:

- 4 cups chicken or vegetable broth
- 8 oz mushrooms (such as straw mushrooms, shiitake mushrooms, or button mushrooms), sliced
- 2 stalks lemongrass, outer layers removed and cut into 2-inch pieces
- 3-4 kaffir lime leaves, torn into pieces (optional)
- 3-4 slices galangal or ginger
- 2-3 Thai bird's eye chilies, crushed (adjust to taste)
- 3 tablespoons fish sauce
- 2 tablespoons lime juice
- 1 tablespoon soy sauce or tamari (optional)
- 1 tablespoon palm sugar or brown sugar (adjust to taste)
- 2 tomatoes, cut into wedges
- 1 small onion, thinly sliced
- Fresh cilantro leaves, for garnish
- Thinly sliced green onions, for garnish
- Optional: Sliced tofu, cooked shrimp, or cooked chicken for added protein
- Optional: Thai chili paste (Nam Prik Pao) for extra heat

Instructions:

1. Prepare the Broth: In a large pot, bring the chicken or vegetable broth to a boil over medium-high heat.
2. Add Lemongrass and Aromatics: Add the lemongrass pieces, torn kaffir lime leaves (if using), slices of galangal or ginger, and crushed Thai bird's eye chilies to the boiling broth. Reduce the heat to medium-low and let the broth simmer for about 5-10 minutes to infuse the flavors.
3. Add Mushrooms and Vegetables: Add the sliced mushrooms, tomato wedges, and thinly sliced onion to the pot. If you're adding protein such as tofu, shrimp, or chicken, add it at this stage as well. Let the soup simmer for another 5-7 minutes, or until the mushrooms are tender.
4. Season the Soup: Stir in the fish sauce, lime juice, soy sauce or tamari (if using), and palm sugar or brown sugar. Taste the soup and adjust the seasoning according to your preference. If you prefer a spicier soup, you can add Thai chili paste (Nam Prik Pao) to increase the heat.
5. Simmer and Serve: Let the soup simmer for a few more minutes to allow the flavors to meld together. Once ready, remove the lemongrass pieces and galangal or ginger slices from the soup.
6. Garnish and Serve: Ladle the hot Tom Yum Soup into serving bowls. Garnish with fresh cilantro leaves and thinly sliced green onions. Serve hot and enjoy!

This Tom Yum Soup with Mushrooms and Lemongrass is best enjoyed immediately as a flavorful and comforting appetizer or main dish. Adjust the ingredients and seasoning according to your taste preferences, and feel free to customize it with your favorite vegetables and protein choices.

Chinese Egg Drop Soup with Spinach

Ingredients:

- 4 cups chicken or vegetable broth
- 2 cups water
- 2 cups fresh spinach leaves, roughly chopped
- 2 large eggs, beaten
- 1 tablespoon soy sauce
- 1 teaspoon sesame oil
- 1 tablespoon cornstarch
- 2 green onions, thinly sliced (for garnish)
- Salt and pepper, to taste

Instructions:

1. Prepare the Broth: In a large pot, bring the chicken or vegetable broth and water to a simmer over medium heat.
2. Add Spinach: Once the broth is simmering, add the chopped spinach leaves to the pot. Let them cook for 1-2 minutes, or until wilted.
3. Season the Soup: In a small bowl, whisk together the beaten eggs, soy sauce, sesame oil, and cornstarch until well combined. Slowly pour the egg mixture into the simmering broth, stirring gently with a fork to create egg ribbons. Let the soup cook for another 1-2 minutes to fully cook the eggs.
4. Taste and Adjust: Taste the soup and season with salt and pepper to your liking. Keep in mind that the soy sauce adds saltiness, so you may not need much additional salt.
5. Garnish and Serve: Ladle the hot soup into serving bowls and garnish with thinly sliced green onions.
6. Enjoy: Serve the Chinese Egg Drop Soup with Spinach hot as a comforting appetizer or light meal.

Feel free to customize this soup by adding other vegetables such as sliced mushrooms, shredded carrots, or bamboo shoots. You can also add cooked chicken, shrimp, or tofu for added protein. Adjust the seasoning and thickness of the soup by adding more or less cornstarch slurry as needed.

Korean Seaweed Soup with Tofu and Shiitake Mushrooms

Ingredients:

- 1 cup dried miyeok (seaweed)
- 4 cups water
- 4 cups vegetable or mushroom broth
- 1 cup sliced shiitake mushrooms
- 1 cup firm tofu, cut into small cubes
- 2 cloves garlic, minced
- 2 tablespoons soy sauce
- 1 tablespoon sesame oil
- Salt and pepper, to taste
- 2 green onions, thinly sliced (for garnish)
- Toasted sesame seeds, for garnish

Instructions:

1. Prepare the Seaweed: Rinse the dried miyeok (seaweed) under cold water to remove any dirt or debris. Place the rinsed miyeok in a large bowl and cover it with water. Let it soak for about 20-30 minutes, or until it becomes soft and rehydrated. Drain the rehydrated miyeok and set it aside.
2. Prepare the Broth: In a large pot, bring the water and vegetable or mushroom broth to a boil over medium-high heat.
3. Add Seaweed and Shiitake Mushrooms: Once the broth is boiling, add the rehydrated miyeok (seaweed) and sliced shiitake mushrooms to the pot. Let them cook for about 5-7 minutes, or until the mushrooms are tender.
4. Add Tofu and Seasonings: Add the cubed tofu, minced garlic, soy sauce, and sesame oil to the pot. Stir gently to combine. Let the soup simmer for another 3-5 minutes to allow the flavors to meld together. Taste the soup and season with salt and pepper as needed.
5. Garnish and Serve: Ladle the hot soup into serving bowls. Garnish with thinly sliced green onions and toasted sesame seeds.
6. Enjoy: Serve the Korean Seaweed Soup with Tofu and Shiitake Mushrooms hot as a comforting and nutritious meal.

Feel free to customize this soup by adding other vegetables such as sliced carrots, spinach, or zucchini. You can also add cooked protein such as shredded chicken or beef if desired. Adjust the seasoning and thickness of the soup according to your taste preferences.

Thai Coconut Curry Soup with Vegetables

Ingredients:

- 1 tablespoon vegetable oil
- 1 small onion, diced
- 2 cloves garlic, minced
- 1 tablespoon fresh ginger, grated
- 2 tablespoons Thai red curry paste
- 1 can (13.5 oz) coconut milk
- 4 cups vegetable broth
- 1 cup sliced mushrooms
- 1 red bell pepper, thinly sliced
- 1 cup broccoli florets
- 1 carrot, thinly sliced
- 1 cup firm tofu, cubed
- 2 tablespoons soy sauce or tamari
- 1 tablespoon brown sugar or coconut sugar
- Juice of 1 lime
- Salt and pepper, to taste
- Fresh cilantro, for garnish
- Cooked rice or rice noodles, for serving (optional)

Instructions:

1. Sauté Aromatics: Heat the vegetable oil in a large pot over medium heat. Add the diced onion, minced garlic, and grated ginger. Sauté for 2-3 minutes, or until the onions are softened and fragrant.
2. Add Curry Paste: Stir in the Thai red curry paste and cook for another minute, stirring constantly to toast the spices and release their flavors.
3. Simmer with Coconut Milk: Pour in the coconut milk and vegetable broth, stirring to combine. Bring the mixture to a simmer.
4. Add Vegetables and Tofu: Add the sliced mushrooms, red bell pepper, broccoli florets, carrot, and cubed tofu to the pot. Let the soup simmer for about 10-15 minutes, or until the vegetables are tender and the tofu is heated through.
5. Season the Soup: Stir in the soy sauce or tamari, brown sugar or coconut sugar, and lime juice. Taste the soup and season with salt and pepper as needed.

6. Garnish and Serve: Ladle the Thai Coconut Curry Soup into serving bowls. Garnish with fresh cilantro leaves. Serve hot as is or over cooked rice or rice noodles, if desired.
7. Enjoy: Enjoy the Thai Coconut Curry Soup with Vegetables as a satisfying and flavorful meal!

Feel free to customize this soup by adding other vegetables such as spinach, snow peas, or green beans. You can also adjust the level of spiciness by adding more or less Thai red curry paste according to your preference. Additionally, you can swap the tofu for cooked chicken, shrimp, or chickpeas for added protein.

Japanese Udon Soup with Bok Choy and Seared Tofu

Ingredients:

- 8 oz udon noodles
- 4 cups vegetable broth
- 2 cups water
- 1 tablespoon soy sauce
- 1 tablespoon mirin (Japanese sweet rice wine)
- 1 tablespoon sesame oil
- 1 tablespoon miso paste
- 2 heads baby bok choy, halved or quartered
- 8 oz firm tofu, sliced into cubes
- 2 green onions, thinly sliced
- 2 cloves garlic, minced
- 1 tablespoon grated ginger
- Sesame seeds, for garnish
- Red pepper flakes, for garnish (optional)
- Salt and pepper, to taste

Instructions:

1. Cook the Udon Noodles: Cook the udon noodles according to the package instructions. Drain and set aside.
2. Prepare the Broth: In a large pot, combine the vegetable broth, water, soy sauce, mirin, sesame oil, miso paste, minced garlic, and grated ginger. Bring the mixture to a simmer over medium heat.
3. Sear the Tofu: Heat a non-stick skillet over medium-high heat. Add a drizzle of oil to the skillet. Once hot, add the tofu cubes in a single layer. Cook for 3-4 minutes on each side, or until golden brown and crispy. Remove from heat and set aside.
4. Add Bok Choy: Once the broth is simmering, add the baby bok choy halves or quarters to the pot. Let them cook for 3-4 minutes, or until tender-crisp.
5. Assemble the Soup: Divide the cooked udon noodles among serving bowls. Ladle the hot broth and bok choy over the noodles.
6. Add Tofu and Garnish: Top each bowl with seared tofu cubes and thinly sliced green onions. Sprinkle with sesame seeds and red pepper flakes, if desired.
7. Serve: Serve the Japanese Udon Soup with Bok Choy and Seared Tofu hot, and enjoy the comforting and flavorful combination of flavors!

Feel free to customize this soup by adding other vegetables such as sliced mushrooms, snow peas, or sliced carrots. You can also adjust the seasoning of the broth by adding more soy sauce, mirin, or miso paste according to your taste preferences. Additionally, you can add a splash of rice vinegar or lime juice for extra acidity.

Soba Noodle Soup with Miso-Glazed Salmon

Ingredients:

For the Miso-Glazed Salmon:

- 2 salmon fillets (about 6 oz each)
- 2 tablespoons white miso paste
- 1 tablespoon soy sauce
- 1 tablespoon mirin (Japanese sweet rice wine)
- 1 tablespoon honey or brown sugar
- 1 teaspoon grated ginger
- 1 garlic clove, minced

For the Soba Noodle Soup:

- 6 cups vegetable or fish broth
- 2 bundles (about 6 oz) soba noodles
- 4 cups baby spinach or chopped spinach leaves
- 2 green onions, thinly sliced
- 1 tablespoon soy sauce
- 1 tablespoon mirin
- 1 tablespoon sesame oil
- 1 teaspoon grated ginger
- 2 cloves garlic, minced
- Salt and pepper, to taste
- Sesame seeds, for garnish
- Thinly sliced nori (seaweed), for garnish (optional)

Instructions:

1. Prepare the Miso-Glazed Salmon:
   - In a small bowl, whisk together the white miso paste, soy sauce, mirin, honey or brown sugar, grated ginger, and minced garlic.
   - Place the salmon fillets in a shallow dish or resealable plastic bag. Pour the miso marinade over the salmon, making sure it's evenly coated. Let it marinate in the refrigerator for at least 30 minutes, or up to 2 hours.
2. Cook the Soba Noodles:

- Bring a pot of water to a boil. Cook the soba noodles according to the package instructions until al dente. Drain and rinse the noodles under cold water to stop the cooking process. Set aside.

3. Prepare the Soup Base:
   - In a large pot, bring the vegetable or fish broth to a simmer over medium heat.
   - Add the thinly sliced green onions, minced garlic, grated ginger, soy sauce, mirin, and sesame oil to the pot. Let the flavors meld together for a few minutes.

4. Cook the Miso-Glazed Salmon:
   - Preheat the oven to 400°F (200°C). Line a baking sheet with parchment paper.
   - Place the marinated salmon fillets on the prepared baking sheet. Bake for 12-15 minutes, or until the salmon is cooked through and flakes easily with a fork.

5. Assemble the Soba Noodle Soup:
   - Add the cooked soba noodles and baby spinach to the pot of simmering broth. Let the spinach wilt and the noodles heat through.
   - Season the soup with salt and pepper to taste. Adjust the seasoning if necessary.
   - Divide the soba noodle soup among serving bowls. Place a piece of miso-glazed salmon on top of each bowl.
   - Garnish with sesame seeds and thinly sliced nori, if desired.

6. Serve:
   - Serve the Soba Noodle Soup with Miso-Glazed Salmon hot and enjoy the comforting blend of flavors!

Feel free to customize this dish by adding other vegetables to the soup, such as sliced mushrooms, bok choy, or shredded carrots. You can also adjust the sweetness and saltiness of the miso glaze according to your taste preferences. Enjoy your homemade Soba Noodle Soup with Miso-Glazed Salmon!

Thai Tom Kha Gai Soup with Chicken and Galangal

Ingredients:

- 4 cups chicken broth
- 1 can (13.5 oz) coconut milk
- 2 cups cooked chicken breast, shredded or thinly sliced
- 1 stalk lemongrass, bruised and cut into pieces
- 3-4 slices galangal or ginger
- 3-4 kaffir lime leaves, torn into pieces
- 2-3 Thai bird's eye chilies, crushed (adjust to taste)
- 1 cup sliced mushrooms (such as straw mushrooms or button mushrooms)
- 1 cup cherry tomatoes, halved
- 1 tablespoon fish sauce
- 1 tablespoon lime juice
- 1 tablespoon palm sugar or brown sugar (adjust to taste)
- Salt, to taste
- Fresh cilantro leaves, for garnish
- Thinly sliced red chili peppers, for garnish (optional)
- Cooked rice, for serving (optional)

Instructions:

1. Prepare the Soup Base: In a large pot, combine the chicken broth and coconut milk. Bring the mixture to a simmer over medium heat.
2. Infuse with Aromatics: Add the bruised lemongrass, slices of galangal or ginger, torn kaffir lime leaves, and crushed Thai bird's eye chilies to the pot. Let the soup simmer for about 5-7 minutes to infuse the flavors into the broth.
3. Add Chicken and Vegetables: Add the cooked chicken breast, sliced mushrooms, and halved cherry tomatoes to the pot. Let them cook for another 5-7 minutes, or until the mushrooms are tender and the chicken is heated through.
4. Season the Soup: Stir in the fish sauce, lime juice, and palm sugar or brown sugar. Taste the soup and adjust the seasoning with salt if needed. The soup should have a balance of salty, sour, and slightly sweet flavors.
5. Simmer and Serve: Let the soup simmer for a few more minutes to allow the flavors to meld together. Once ready, remove the lemongrass stalks, galangal or ginger slices, and kaffir lime leaves from the soup.
6. Garnish and Serve: Ladle the hot Tom Kha Gai Soup into serving bowls. Garnish with fresh cilantro leaves and thinly sliced red chili peppers, if desired.
7. Serve: Serve the Thai Tom Kha Gai Soup with Chicken and Galangal hot, and enjoy the fragrant and flavorful combination of ingredients! Optionally, serve with cooked rice on the side for a heartier meal.

Feel free to adjust the ingredients and seasonings according to your taste preferences. You can add more or fewer Thai bird's eye chilies to adjust the spiciness level, and you can also add other vegetables such as sliced bell peppers or bamboo shoots for additional flavor and texture.

Chinese Wonton Soup with Shrimp and Bok Choy

Ingredients:

For the Wontons:

- 1/2 pound shrimp, peeled, deveined, and finely chopped
- 1/4 cup finely chopped bok choy
- 2 green onions, finely chopped
- 2 cloves garlic, minced
- 1 teaspoon grated ginger
- 1 tablespoon soy sauce
- 1 teaspoon sesame oil
- 1/2 teaspoon salt
- 1/4 teaspoon black pepper
- 24 square wonton wrappers

For the Soup:

- 6 cups chicken broth
- 2 cups water
- 2 cups baby bok choy, chopped
- 2 green onions, sliced
- 1 tablespoon soy sauce
- 1 teaspoon sesame oil
- Salt and pepper, to taste

Instructions:

1. Prepare the Wonton Filling:
    - In a mixing bowl, combine the chopped shrimp, bok choy, green onions, garlic, ginger, soy sauce, sesame oil, salt, and black pepper. Mix well to combine.
2. Assemble the Wontons:
    - Place a small spoonful of the shrimp mixture in the center of each wonton wrapper.
    - Moisten the edges of the wrapper with water, then fold the wrapper over the filling to form a triangle. Press the edges to seal, making sure to remove any air pockets.
3. Cook the Wontons:
    - Bring a large pot of water to a boil. Carefully drop the wontons into the boiling water, working in batches if necessary to avoid overcrowding.

- Cook the wontons for 3-4 minutes, or until they float to the surface and are cooked through. Remove them with a slotted spoon and set aside.
4. Prepare the Soup:
   - In a separate pot, bring the chicken broth and water to a simmer over medium heat.
   - Add the chopped baby bok choy, sliced green onions, soy sauce, and sesame oil to the pot. Let the vegetables cook for 2-3 minutes, or until they are tender-crisp.
5. Assemble the Soup:
   - Divide the cooked wontons among serving bowls.
   - Ladle the hot soup over the wontons.
   - Season the soup with salt and pepper to taste.
6. Serve:
   - Serve the Chinese Wonton Soup with Shrimp and Bok Choy hot, garnished with additional sliced green onions if desired.
7. Enjoy!

Feel free to customize this soup by adding other vegetables such as sliced mushrooms or shredded carrots. You can also adjust the seasoning of the soup by adding more soy sauce or sesame oil according to your taste preferences. Enjoy your homemade Wonton Soup!

Vietnamese Bun Rieu Soup with Crab and Tomatoes

Ingredients:

For the Crab Cake:

- 1 pound fresh crab meat (or canned crab meat)
- 1 egg
- 1/4 cup breadcrumbs
- 2 cloves garlic, minced
- 2 green onions, finely chopped
- 1 tablespoon fish sauce
- 1 teaspoon sugar
- 1/2 teaspoon ground black pepper

For the Soup:

- 8 cups chicken broth
- 2 cups water
- 2 tomatoes, chopped
- 1 onion, chopped
- 3 cloves garlic, minced
- 1 tablespoon shrimp paste (optional)
- 1 tablespoon fish sauce
- 1 tablespoon sugar
- 1 teaspoon ground annatto (optional, for color)
- 1/2 teaspoon ground black pepper
- Salt, to taste

For Serving:

- 1 pound rice vermicelli noodles (bun)
- Fresh herbs (such as cilantro, mint, and Thai basil)
- Bean sprouts
- Lime wedges
- Sliced chili peppers (optional)

Instructions:

1. Prepare the Crab Cake:
   - In a mixing bowl, combine the crab meat, egg, breadcrumbs, minced garlic, chopped green onions, fish sauce, sugar, and black pepper. Mix well until everything is evenly combined.
   - Shape the mixture into small crab cakes, about 1-2 inches in diameter. Set aside.
2. Make the Soup Base:
   - In a large pot, combine the chicken broth and water. Bring to a simmer over medium heat.
   - Add the chopped tomatoes, chopped onion, minced garlic, shrimp paste (if using), fish sauce, sugar, ground annatto (if using), and black pepper to the pot. Let the soup simmer for about 15-20 minutes to allow the flavors to meld together.
3. Cook the Crab Cakes:
   - Carefully drop the crab cakes into the simmering soup. Let them cook for about 5-7 minutes, or until they are cooked through and firm.
4. Prepare the Noodles:
   - While the soup is simmering, cook the rice vermicelli noodles according to the package instructions. Drain and rinse them under cold water to stop the cooking process. Set aside.
5. Assemble the Soup:
   - Divide the cooked rice vermicelli noodles among serving bowls.
   - Ladle the hot soup and crab cakes over the noodles.
6. Serve:
   - Serve the Vietnamese Bun Rieu Soup with Crab and Tomatoes hot, garnished with fresh herbs, bean sprouts, lime wedges, and sliced chili peppers if desired.
7. Enjoy!

Feel free to customize this soup by adding other ingredients such as tofu puffs, shrimp, or pork slices. Adjust the seasoning according to your taste preferences. Enjoy your homemade Bun Rieu Soup!

Korean Kimchi Soup with Tofu and Spinach

Ingredients:

- 2 cups chopped kimchi (with juice)
- 1 cup firm tofu, cut into cubes
- 2 cups baby spinach, washed
- 4 cups vegetable or beef broth
- 1 onion, thinly sliced
- 2 cloves garlic, minced
- 2 green onions, chopped
- 1 tablespoon sesame oil
- 1 tablespoon gochujang (Korean chili paste)
- 1 tablespoon soy sauce
- 1 tablespoon rice vinegar (optional)
- 1 teaspoon sugar (optional)
- Salt and pepper, to taste
- Cooked rice, for serving
- Toasted sesame seeds, for garnish
- Thinly sliced green onions, for garnish

Instructions:

1. Prepare the Soup Base:
    - In a large pot, heat the sesame oil over medium heat. Add the minced garlic and sliced onions. Sauté until the onions are soft and translucent.
2. Add Kimchi and Broth:
    - Add the chopped kimchi (with its juice) to the pot. Stir and cook for a few minutes to soften the kimchi and release its flavors.
    - Pour in the vegetable or beef broth. Bring the mixture to a simmer.
3. Season the Soup:
    - Stir in the gochujang and soy sauce. If desired, add the rice vinegar and sugar for a balanced flavor. Taste the soup and adjust the seasoning with salt and pepper as needed.
4. Add Tofu and Spinach:
    - Gently add the cubed tofu to the simmering soup. Let it cook for a few minutes to absorb the flavors.
    - Add the baby spinach to the pot. Stir and cook until the spinach wilts.
5. Serve:
    - Ladle the hot Kimchi Soup with Tofu and Spinach into serving bowls.
    - Garnish with toasted sesame seeds and thinly sliced green onions.
    - Serve with cooked rice on the side.

6. Enjoy!

Feel free to customize this soup by adding other ingredients such as mushrooms, zucchini, or seafood. You can also adjust the spiciness level by adding more or less gochujang according to your preference. Enjoy your homemade Kimchi Soup!

Japanese Clear Soup with Enoki Mushrooms and Daikon Radish

Ingredients:

- 6 cups water or vegetable broth
- 1 small daikon radish, peeled and thinly sliced
- 1 cup enoki mushrooms, bottom trimmed and separated into individual strands
- 2 green onions, thinly sliced
- 2 tablespoons soy sauce
- 1 tablespoon mirin (Japanese sweet rice wine)
- 1 tablespoon sake (Japanese rice wine) or dry sherry
- Salt, to taste
- Fresh cilantro leaves, for garnish (optional)

Instructions:

1. Prepare the Daikon Radish:
    - Peel the daikon radish and slice it thinly into rounds. You can also use a mandoline slicer for uniform slices.
2. Prepare the Soup Base:
    - In a large pot, bring the water or vegetable broth to a simmer over medium heat.
    - Add the sliced daikon radish to the pot. Let it cook for about 5 minutes, or until it starts to soften.
3. Add Enoki Mushrooms and Green Onions:
    - Add the separated strands of enoki mushrooms and thinly sliced green onions to the pot.
    - Let the soup simmer for another 2-3 minutes, or until the mushrooms are tender and the green onions are wilted.
4. Season the Soup:
    - Stir in the soy sauce, mirin, and sake (or dry sherry) to the pot. Taste the soup and adjust the seasoning with salt if needed. Be careful not to oversalt, as the soy sauce already adds saltiness.
5. Simmer and Serve:
    - Let the soup simmer for a few more minutes to allow the flavors to meld together.
    - Once ready, remove the pot from the heat.
6. Garnish and Serve:
    - Ladle the hot Japanese Clear Soup with Enoki Mushrooms and Daikon Radish into serving bowls.
    - Garnish with fresh cilantro leaves if desired.
7. Enjoy!

Feel free to customize this soup by adding other ingredients such as tofu, thinly sliced carrots, or shiitake mushrooms. You can also adjust the seasoning by adding more soy sauce or mirin according to your taste preferences. Enjoy your homemade Japanese Clear Soup!

Thai Tom Yum Goong Soup with Shrimp and Lemongrass

Ingredients:

- 4 cups shrimp or seafood broth
- 2 cups water
- 1 stalk lemongrass, bruised and chopped into pieces
- 3-4 kaffir lime leaves, torn into pieces
- 2-3 Thai bird's eye chilies, crushed (adjust to taste)
- 1-inch piece galangal or ginger, sliced
- 8-10 medium-sized shrimp, peeled and deveined
- 1 cup sliced mushrooms (such as straw mushrooms or button mushrooms)
- 1 tomato, cut into wedges
- 1 small onion, thinly sliced
- 2 tablespoons fish sauce
- 2 tablespoons lime juice
- 1 tablespoon sugar
- Salt, to taste
- Fresh cilantro leaves, for garnish
- Thinly sliced red chili peppers, for garnish (optional)

Instructions:

1. Prepare the Soup Base:
    - In a large pot, combine the shrimp or seafood broth and water. Bring to a simmer over medium heat.
    - Add the lemongrass, kaffir lime leaves, crushed Thai bird's eye chilies, and sliced galangal or ginger to the pot. Let the soup simmer for about 5-7 minutes to infuse the flavors into the broth.
2. Add Shrimp and Vegetables:
    - Add the peeled and deveined shrimp to the simmering broth. Let them cock for about 2-3 minutes, or until they turn pink and opaque.
    - Stir in the sliced mushrooms, tomato wedges, and thinly sliced onion. Let the vegetables cook for another 2-3 minutes, or until they are tender.
3. Season the Soup:
    - Stir in the fish sauce, lime juice, and sugar. Taste the soup and adjust the seasoning with salt if needed. The soup should have a balance of salty, sour, and slightly sweet flavors.
4. Simmer and Serve:
    - Let the soup simmer for a few more minutes to allow the flavors to meld together.
    - Once ready, remove the lemongrass stalks, kaffir lime leaves, and galangal or ginger slices from the soup.

5. Garnish and Serve:
    - Ladle the hot Tom Yum Goong Soup with Shrimp and Lemongrass into serving bowls.
    - Garnish with fresh cilantro leaves and thinly sliced red chili peppers if desired.
6. Enjoy!

Feel free to customize this soup by adding other ingredients such as tofu, sliced bell peppers, or bamboo shoots. Adjust the spiciness level by adding more or fewer Thai bird's eye chilies according to your preference. Enjoy your homemade Tom Yum Goong Soup!

Chinese Hot Pot Soup with Sliced Beef and Napa Cabbage

Ingredients:

For the Broth:

- 6 cups beef or chicken broth
- 2 cups water
- 3 slices ginger
- 2 cloves garlic, smashed
- 2 green onions, chopped
- 1 star anise
- 1 cinnamon stick
- 2 tablespoons soy sauce
- 1 tablespoon rice wine or dry sherry
- Salt, to taste

For the Hot Pot Ingredients:

- 1 pound thinly sliced beef (such as sirloin or ribeye)
- 1 small Napa cabbage, cut into bite-sized pieces
- 1 package enoki mushrooms, bottom trimmed
- 1 package shiitake mushrooms, stems removed and caps sliced
- 1 block tofu, sliced
- 1 bunch baby bok choy, separated into leaves
- 1 package shirataki noodles (optional)
- Dipping sauces (such as soy sauce, sesame oil, and chili sauce), for serving

Instructions:

1. Prepare the Broth:
    - In a large pot, combine the beef or chicken broth, water, ginger slices, smashed garlic cloves, chopped green onions, star anise, and cinnamon stick.
    - Add the soy sauce and rice wine or dry sherry to the pot. Bring the mixture to a simmer over medium heat.
    - Let the broth simmer for about 20-30 minutes to allow the flavors to meld together. Season with salt to taste.

2. Prepare the Hot Pot Ingredients:
   - Arrange the thinly sliced beef, Napa cabbage, enoki mushrooms, shiitake mushrooms, tofu slices, baby bok choy, and shirataki noodles (if using) on a platter or in individual bowls.
3. Set Up the Hot Pot:
   - Place a portable burner or electric hot pot in the center of the dining table.
   - Pour the simmering broth into the hot pot.
4. Cook the Ingredients:
   - Each diner can use chopsticks or a small strainer to cook their desired ingredients in the hot pot.
   - Dip the thinly sliced beef into the hot broth and cook for a few seconds until it turns opaque. Remove and dip into your favorite dipping sauce before eating.
   - Repeat the process with the Napa cabbage, mushrooms, tofu, baby bok choy, and shirataki noodles, cooking them until tender.
5. Serve:
   - Serve the cooked ingredients with dipping sauces on the side.
   - Enjoy the Chinese Hot Pot Soup with Sliced Beef and Napa Cabbage as a fun and interactive meal with family and friends!

Feel free to customize this hot pot by adding other ingredients such as seafood, fish balls, dumplings, or different types of vegetables. Adjust the seasoning of the broth according to your taste preferences. Enjoy your homemade hot pot experience!

Indonesian Soto Ayam Soup with Chicken and Turmeric

Ingredients:

For the Soup:

- 1 whole chicken (about 3-4 pounds), cut into pieces
- 8 cups water
- 2 stalks lemongrass, bruised and tied into knots
- 3 kaffir lime leaves
- 4 cloves garlic, minced
- 1-inch piece ginger, thinly sliced
- 1-inch piece fresh turmeric, thinly sliced (or 1 tablespoon ground turmeric)
- 2 bay leaves
- Salt, to taste
- Ground white pepper, to taste
- 2 tablespoons vegetable oil
- Cooked rice, for serving
- Fried shallots, for garnish
- Sliced green onions, for garnish
- Hard-boiled eggs, halved, for serving
- Lime wedges, for serving
- Sambal or chili paste, for serving (optional)

For the Spice Paste (Bumbu):

- 4 shallots, peeled
- 3 cloves garlic, peeled
- 1-inch piece ginger, peeled
- 1-inch piece fresh turmeric, peeled (or 1 teaspoon ground turmeric)
- 2 candlenuts or macadamia nuts (optional)
- 2 teaspoons coriander seeds
- 1 teaspoon cumin seeds
- 1/2 teaspoon fennel seeds
- 1/2 teaspoon black peppercorns
- 2 tablespoons vegetable oil

Instructions:

1. Prepare the Spice Paste (Bumbu):

- In a blender or food processor, combine all the ingredients for the spice paste (shallots, garlic, ginger, turmeric, candlenuts or macadamia nuts, coriander seeds, cumin seeds, fennel seeds, and black peppercorns). Blend until smooth.
2. Cook the Chicken:
    - In a large pot, heat 2 tablespoons of vegetable oil over medium heat. Add the minced garlic and sliced ginger, and cook until fragrant, about 1-2 minutes.
    - Add the spice paste (bumbu) to the pot and cook, stirring frequently, for another 3-4 minutes until fragrant.
    - Add the chicken pieces to the pot and cook until they are lightly browned on all sides.
    - Pour in the water and add the lemongrass knots, kaffir lime leaves, fresh turmeric slices (or ground turmeric), bay leaves, salt, and white pepper.
    - Bring the soup to a boil, then reduce the heat to low and let it simmer, covered, for about 30-40 minutes or until the chicken is tender and cooked through.
3. Prepare the Garnishes:
    - While the soup is simmering, prepare the garnishes. Cook the rice and hard-boiled eggs if you haven't already done so. Slice the green onions and halve the hard-boiled eggs. Prepare the lime wedges and fried shallots.
4. Serve:
    - Once the chicken is cooked through and tender, remove the chicken pieces from the soup and shred the meat using two forks. Discard the bones and return the shredded chicken meat to the soup.
    - Taste the soup and adjust the seasoning with salt and white pepper if needed.
    - To serve, place a portion of cooked rice in serving bowls. Ladle the hot Soto Ayam Soup over the rice.
    - Garnish each bowl with fried shallots, sliced green onions, a halved hard-boiled egg, and a lime wedge on the side.
    - Serve the Indonesian Soto Ayam Soup with Chicken and Turmeric hot, along with sambal or chili paste on the side for extra heat if desired.

Enjoy your delicious homemade Indonesian Soto Ayam Soup with Chicken and Turmeric!

Vietnamese Canh Chua Soup with Pineapple and Fish

Ingredients:

- 4 cups fish or vegetable broth
- 2 cups water
- 1 pound white fish fillets (such as tilapia or catfish), cut into bite-sized pieces
- 1 cup pineapple chunks (fresh or canned)
- 1 medium tomato, cut into wedges
- 1/2 cup okra, trimmed and sliced
- 1/2 cup bean sprouts
- 2-3 Thai bird's eye chilies, sliced (optional, adjust to taste)
- 2 tablespoons tamarind paste or pulp
- 2 tablespoons fish sauce
- 1 tablespoon sugar
- 2 cloves garlic, minced
- 1 shallot, thinly sliced
- 1 stalk lemongrass, bruised and chopped into pieces
- 2 kaffir lime leaves, torn into pieces
- Handful of fresh cilantro leaves, for garnish
- Handful of fresh mint leaves, for garnish
- Lime wedges, for serving
- Cooked rice, for serving

Instructions:

1. Prepare the Broth:
    - In a large pot, combine the fish or vegetable broth and water. Bring to a simmer over medium heat.
2. Add Aromatics:
    - Add the minced garlic, sliced shallot, chopped lemongrass, and torn kaffir lime leaves to the pot. Let the broth simmer for about 5 minutes to infuse the flavors.
3. Add Pineapple and Tamarind:
    - Add the pineapple chunks to the pot. If using tamarind pulp, dissolve it in a little warm water and strain out any seeds or fibers. Add the tamarind liquid to the pot.
4. Season the Soup:
    - Stir in the fish sauce and sugar. Taste the broth and adjust the seasoning as needed, adding more fish sauce for saltiness, sugar for sweetness, or tamarind for sourness.
5. Cook the Fish and Vegetables:
    - Add the sliced okra, tomato wedges, and fish pieces to the pot. Let them cook for about 5-7 minutes, or until the fish is cooked through and the vegetables are tender.
6. Add Bean Sprouts and Chilies:

          - Add the bean sprouts and sliced Thai bird's eye chilies to the pot. Let them cook for another minute.
     7. Garnish and Serve:
          - Ladle the hot Canh Chua Soup into serving bowls. Garnish with fresh cilantro and mint leaves.
          - Serve with lime wedges and cooked rice on the side.
     8. Enjoy!

Feel free to adjust the ingredients and seasonings according to your taste preferences. You can also add other vegetables such as taro stems, celery, or zucchini. Enjoy your delicious homemade Vietnamese Canh Chua Soup with Pineapple and Fish!

Japanese Miso Ramen Soup with Shiitake Mushrooms and Spinach

Ingredients:

For the Ramen Broth:

- 6 cups vegetable or chicken broth
- 2 cups water
- 4 cloves garlic, minced
- 1-inch piece ginger, thinly sliced
- 2 tablespoons soy sauce
- 2 tablespoons mirin (Japanese sweet rice wine)
- 2 tablespoons sake (Japanese rice wine) or dry sherry
- 2 tablespoons miso paste (white or red)
- 2 tablespoons sesame oil
- Salt, to taste
- Ground black pepper, to taste

For the Ramen Soup:

- 8 ounces ramen noodles
- 1 cup sliced shiitake mushrooms
- 2 cups fresh spinach leaves
- 2 green onions, thinly sliced
- 2 boiled eggs, halved (optional)
- Nori sheets, for garnish (optional)
- Sesame seeds, for garnish (optional)

Instructions:

1. Prepare the Ramen Broth:
    - In a large pot, combine the vegetable or chicken broth, water, minced garlic, thinly sliced ginger, soy sauce, mirin, and sake (or dry sherry).
    - Bring the broth to a simmer over medium heat and let it cook for about 15-20 minutes to infuse the flavors.
2. Cook the Ramen Noodles:
    - While the broth is simmering, cook the ramen noodles according to the package instructions. Drain and rinse the noodles under cold water to stop the cooking process. Set aside.
3. Prepare the Shiitake Mushrooms and Spinach:

- In a separate pan, heat a little sesame oil over medium heat. Add the sliced shiitake mushrooms and cook for 2-3 minutes, or until they are tender.
- Add the fresh spinach leaves to the pan and cook for another 1-2 minutes, or until they are wilted. Remove from heat and set aside.

4. Finish the Ramen Broth:
   - Once the broth has simmered and the flavors have melded together, remove the pot from the heat.
   - Add the miso paste to the broth and stir until it is fully dissolved. Taste the broth and adjust the seasoning with salt and black pepper as needed.
5. Assemble the Ramen Soup:
   - Divide the cooked ramen noodles among serving bowls.
   - Ladle the hot ramen broth over the noodles.
   - Top each bowl with the cooked shiitake mushrooms and spinach.
6. Garnish and Serve:
   - Garnish each bowl with sliced green onions, halved boiled eggs (if using), nori sheets, and sesame seeds.
   - Serve the Japanese Miso Ramen Soup with Shiitake Mushrooms and Spinach hot and enjoy!

Feel free to customize this ramen soup by adding other toppings such as sliced bamboo shoots, corn kernels, or marinated tofu. Adjust the spiciness level by adding a dash of chili oil or hot sauce if desired. Enjoy your delicious homemade ramen soup!

Thai Spicy Noodle Soup with Shrimp and Rice Noodles

Ingredients:

For the Soup Base:

- 4 cups shrimp or seafood broth
- 2 cups water
- 2 stalks lemongrass, bruised and chopped into pieces
- 4 kaffir lime leaves, torn into pieces
- 4 cloves garlic, minced
- 1-inch piece galangal or ginger, sliced
- 4-6 Thai bird's eye chilies, crushed (adjust to taste)
- 2 tablespoons fish sauce
- 2 tablespoons lime juice
- 1 tablespoon sugar
- 1 cup coconut milk
- Salt, to taste

For the Soup Toppings:

- 8 ounces rice noodles (pad Thai noodles or vermicelli noodles)
- 1 pound large shrimp, peeled and deveined
- 1 cup cherry tomatoes, halved
- 1 cup straw mushrooms, halved
- 1/2 cup sliced bell peppers (red or green)
- Handful of cilantro leaves, for garnish
- Lime wedges, for serving

Instructions:

1. Prepare the Soup Base:
   - In a large pot, combine the shrimp or seafood broth, water, lemongrass, torn kaffir lime leaves, minced garlic, sliced galangal or ginger, and crushed Thai bird's eye chilies.
   - Bring the mixture to a simmer over medium heat and let it cook for about 10-15 minutes to infuse the flavors.
2. Cook the Rice Noodles:

- While the soup base is simmering, cook the rice noodles according to the package instructions. Drain and rinse them under cold water to stop the cooking process. Set aside.
3. Add Coconut Milk and Seasonings:
    - Stir in the fish sauce, lime juice, sugar, and coconut milk to the pot. Let the soup simmer for another 5 minutes to combine the flavors.
    - Taste the soup and adjust the seasoning with salt if needed.
4. Add Soup Toppings:
    - Add the peeled and deveined shrimp, halved cherry tomatoes, halved straw mushrooms, and sliced bell peppers to the pot.
    - Let the soup simmer for about 3-5 minutes, or until the shrimp are pink and cooked through.
5. Assemble the Soup:
    - Divide the cooked rice noodles among serving bowls.
    - Ladle the hot Thai Spicy Noodle Soup with Shrimp over the noodles.
6. Garnish and Serve:
    - Garnish each bowl with a handful of cilantro leaves.
    - Serve the soup hot with lime wedges on the side.
7. Enjoy!

Feel free to customize this spicy noodle soup by adding other ingredients such as tofu, mussels, or squid. Adjust the spiciness level by adding more or fewer Thai bird's eye chilies according to your preference. Enjoy your homemade Thai Spicy Noodle Soup with Shrimp and Rice Noodles!

Chinese Corn Soup with Chicken and Scallions

Ingredients:

- 4 cups chicken broth
- 1 cup water
- 1 cup cooked chicken breast, shredded or diced
- 1 can (about 15 ounces) creamed corn
- 1 cup corn kernels (fresh, frozen, or canned)
- 2 eggs, lightly beaten
- 2 tablespoons soy sauce
- 1 tablespoon rice vinegar
- 1 tablespoon cornstarch, dissolved in 2 tablespoons water
- 2-3 green onions (scallions), thinly sliced
- Salt and pepper, to taste
- Sesame oil, for drizzling (optional)
- Toasted sesame seeds, for garnish (optional)

Instructions:

1. Prepare the Soup Base:
    - In a large pot, bring the chicken broth and water to a simmer over medium heat.
2. Add Chicken and Corn:
    - Add the cooked chicken breast, creamed corn, and corn kernels to the pot. Stir to combine.
3. Season the Soup:
    - Stir in the soy sauce and rice vinegar. Taste the soup and adjust the seasoning with salt and pepper as needed.
4. Thicken the Soup:
    - Slowly pour the beaten eggs into the simmering soup while stirring gently with a fork or chopsticks. This will create delicate egg ribbons in the soup.
    - Once the eggs are cooked, slowly pour the cornstarch mixture into the soup while stirring continuously. This will help thicken the soup slightly.
5. Finish and Serve:
    - Stir in most of the sliced green onions, reserving some for garnish.
    - Let the soup simmer for another minute or two to allow the flavors to meld together.
    - Taste the soup and adjust the seasoning if needed.
    - Ladle the hot Chinese Corn Soup with Chicken and Scallions into serving bowls.
6. Garnish and Serve:
    - Garnish each bowl of soup with a drizzle of sesame oil, if desired, and a sprinkle of toasted sesame seeds.
    - Scatter the reserved sliced green onions over the top.

- Serve the soup hot as an appetizer or a light meal.

Feel free to customize this soup by adding other ingredients such as tofu, shrimp, or additional vegetables like diced carrots or peas. Adjust the thickness of the soup by adding more or less cornstarch mixture according to your preference. Enjoy your delicious homemade Chinese Corn Soup with Chicken and Scallions!

Korean Doenjang Jjigae Soup with Tofu and Zucchini

Ingredients:

- 4 cups water or vegetable broth
- 1/4 cup doenjang (Korean fermented soybean paste)
- 1 tablespoon gochujang (Korean chili paste)
- 1 onion, sliced
- 2 cloves garlic, minced
- 1 zucchini, sliced
- 1 package (about 14 ounces) firm tofu, cut into cubes
- 2 green onions, sliced
- 1 tablespoon sesame oil
- Optional: 1 tablespoon dried anchovies or kelp for extra flavor (remove before serving)
- Optional: Sliced mushrooms, such as shiitake or button mushrooms
- Optional: Sliced chili peppers for extra spice

Instructions:

1. Prepare the Soup Base:
    - In a large pot, bring the water or vegetable broth to a boil over medium heat.
    - If using dried anchovies or kelp, add them to the pot and let them simmer for 5-10 minutes to infuse the broth with flavor. Remove and discard the anchovies or kelp.
2. Add Aromatics and Paste:
    - Add the sliced onion, minced garlic, and sliced zucchini to the pot.
    - Stir in the doenjang and gochujang until they are dissolved into the broth, creating a flavorful base for the soup.
3. Simmer the Soup:
    - Let the soup simmer for about 10-15 minutes, or until the vegetables are tender and the flavors have melded together.
4. Add Tofu and Green Onions:
    - Carefully add the cubed tofu to the simmering soup.
    - Stir in the sliced green onions and optional sliced mushrooms and chili peppers, if using.
5. Finish and Serve:

- Let the soup simmer for another 5 minutes to heat the tofu through.
- Drizzle sesame oil over the soup just before serving for added flavor.
- Taste the soup and adjust the seasoning if needed, adding more doenjang or gochujang according to your taste preferences.

6. Serve Hot:
    - Ladle the hot Doenjang Jjigae Soup with Tofu and Zucchini into serving bowls.
    - Serve the soup hot as a comforting and nutritious meal.

Feel free to customize this soup by adding other ingredients such as spinach, kale, or seafood like clams or shrimp. Adjust the spiciness level by adding more or less gochujang and chili peppers according to your preference. Enjoy your homemade Korean Doenjang Jjigae Soup with Tofu and Zucchini!

Japanese Sukiyaki Soup with Thinly Sliced Beef and Noodles

Ingredients:

- 1/2 pound thinly sliced beef (such as ribeye or sirloin)
- 6 cups dashi broth or beef broth
- 1/4 cup soy sauce
- 1/4 cup mirin (Japanese sweet rice wine)
- 2 tablespoons sugar
- 1 onion, thinly sliced
- 2 cups sliced shiitake mushrooms
- 1 block firm tofu, cut into cubes
- 1 bunch spinach, stems removed
- 4 ounces shirataki noodles or udon noodles
- 4 green onions, cut into 2-inch lengths
- 4-6 shirataki or konjac noodles (optional)
- 1 tablespoon vegetable oil
- Cooked rice, for serving
- Sesame seeds, for garnish (optional)

Instructions:

1. Prepare the Ingredients:
   - If using shirataki or konjac noodles, rinse them under cold water and drain well. Set aside.
   - In a large pot or skillet, heat the vegetable oil over medium heat.
2. Cook the Beef:
   - Add the thinly sliced beef to the pot and cook until browned, about 1-2 minutes per side. Remove the beef from the pot and set aside.
3. Make the Soup Base:
   - In the same pot, add the dashi broth (or beef broth), soy sauce, mirin, and sugar. Stir to combine and bring to a simmer.
4. Add Vegetables and Tofu:
   - Add the sliced onion and shiitake mushrooms to the pot. Let them cook for a few minutes until slightly softened.
   - Add the tofu cubes, spinach, green onions, and cooked beef back into the pot. Let the soup simmer for another 5 minutes to allow the flavors to meld together.
5. Cook the Noodles:
   - While the soup is simmering, cook the shirataki noodles (or udon noodles) according to the package instructions. Drain well and set aside.
6. Assemble the Soup:
   - Divide the cooked noodles among serving bowls.

- Ladle the hot Sukiyaki Soup with Thinly Sliced Beef and Vegetables over the noodles.
7. Garnish and Serve:
    - Garnish each bowl with sesame seeds, if desired.
    - Serve the soup hot with cooked rice on the side.

Feel free to customize this Sukiyaki soup by adding other ingredients such as mushrooms, cabbage, or tofu varieties like silken tofu. Adjust the sweetness and saltiness of the soup base according to your taste preferences. Enjoy your homemade Japanese Sukiyaki Soup with Thinly Sliced Beef and Noodles!

Vietnamese Bun Bo Hue Soup with Spicy Beef and Rice Noodles

Ingredients:

For the Broth:

- 8 cups beef broth
- 2 cups water
- 1 onion, peeled and halved
- 3 cloves garlic, smashed
- 2 stalks lemongrass, bruised and cut into pieces
- 2-3 dried Thai bird's eye chilies
- 2 tablespoons fish sauce
- 1 tablespoon shrimp paste (optional)
- 1 tablespoon sugar
- 1 tablespoon annatto seeds (optional, for color)
- Salt, to taste

For the Spicy Beef:

- 1 pound beef brisket or shank, thinly sliced
- 1 tablespoon vegetable oil
- 2 tablespoons chili oil or chili paste
- 1 tablespoon paprika
- 1 tablespoon minced lemongrass
- 1 tablespoon minced garlic
- 1 tablespoon minced shallots
- 1 tablespoon fish sauce
- Salt and pepper, to taste

For Serving:

- Rice vermicelli noodles, cooked according to package instructions
- Bean sprouts
- Fresh herbs (Thai basil, cilantro, mint)
- Lime wedges
- Sliced green onions
- Thinly sliced onions
- Sliced chili peppers (optional)
- Shrimp paste (optional)

Instructions:

1. Prepare the Broth:
   - In a large pot, combine the beef broth, water, onion halves, smashed garlic cloves, lemongrass pieces, dried Thai bird's eye chilies, fish sauce, shrimp paste (if using), sugar, and annatto seeds (if using).
   - Bring the mixture to a boil over high heat. Reduce the heat to low and let it simmer, covered, for about 1-2 hours to infuse the flavors. Skim off any foam or impurities that rise to the surface.
2. Prepare the Spicy Beef:
   - In a bowl, combine the thinly sliced beef brisket or shank with vegetable oil, chili oil or chili paste, paprika, minced lemongrass, minced garlic, minced shallots, fish sauce, salt, and pepper. Mix well to coat the beef evenly.
   - Heat a skillet or wok over high heat. Add the marinated beef and cook for 3-4 minutes, or until browned and cooked through. Set aside.
3. Assemble the Soup:
   - Strain the broth to remove the solids. Discard the solids and return the strained broth to the pot.
   - Bring the broth back to a simmer over medium heat. Taste and adjust the seasoning with more fish sauce, sugar, or salt if needed.
   - Divide the cooked rice vermicelli noodles among serving bowls. Top with the cooked spicy beef slices.
4. Serve:
   - Ladle the hot Bun Bo Hue Soup broth over the noodles and beef.
   - Serve the soup hot, accompanied by bean sprouts, fresh herbs, lime wedges, sliced green onions, thinly sliced onions, sliced chili peppers (if using), and shrimp paste on the side for diners to customize their bowls according to their taste preferences.

Enjoy your delicious homemade Vietnamese Bun Bo Hue Soup with Spicy Beef and Rice Noodles!

Thai Green Curry Soup with Chicken and Eggplant

Ingredients:

For the Green Curry Paste:

- 4 green Thai chilies (adjust to taste)
- 2 shallots, peeled and chopped
- 4 cloves garlic, peeled
- 1-inch piece ginger, peeled and chopped
- 1 stalk lemongrass, white part only, chopped
- 2 tablespoons cilantro stems, chopped
- 1 tablespoon shrimp paste (optional)
- 1 tablespoon ground coriander
- 1 teaspoon ground cumin
- 1 teaspoon ground white pepper
- 1 tablespoon fish sauce

For the Soup:

- 2 tablespoons vegetable oil
- 2 boneless, skinless chicken breasts, thinly sliced
- 1 can (14 ounces) coconut milk
- 2 cups chicken broth
- 1 small eggplant, diced
- 1 red bell pepper, thinly sliced
- 1 cup sliced bamboo shoots (optional)
- 2 tablespoons fish sauce (adjust to taste)
- 1 tablespoon sugar
- Juice of 1 lime
- Salt, to taste
- Fresh basil or Thai basil leaves, for garnish
- Cooked rice or rice noodles, for serving

Instructions:

1. Prepare the Green Curry Paste:

- In a blender or food processor, combine all the ingredients for the green curry paste: green Thai chilies, shallots, garlic, ginger, lemongrass, cilantro stems, shrimp paste (if using), ground coriander, ground cumin, ground white pepper, and fish sauce.
- Blend until a smooth paste forms. Set aside.

2. Cook the Chicken:
   - In a large pot or wok, heat the vegetable oil over medium heat. Add the sliced chicken breasts and cook until they are no longer pink.
3. Add the Green Curry Paste:
   - Add 2-3 tablespoons of the prepared green curry paste (adjust to taste) to the pot with the cooked chicken. Stir-fry for 1-2 minutes until fragrant.
4. Make the Soup:
   - Pour in the coconut milk and chicken broth. Stir to combine.
   - Add the diced eggplant, sliced red bell pepper, and sliced bamboo shoots (if using) to the pot.
   - Season the soup with fish sauce, sugar, and lime juice. Stir well to combine.
   - Let the soup simmer for about 10-15 minutes, or until the vegetables are tender and the flavors have melded together.
5. Adjust Seasoning and Serve:
   - Taste the soup and adjust the seasoning with salt, fish sauce, sugar, or lime juice as needed.
   - Ladle the hot Thai Green Curry Soup with Chicken and Eggplant into serving bowls.
   - Garnish each bowl with fresh basil or Thai basil leaves.
   - Serve the soup hot, accompanied by cooked rice or rice noodles on the side.

Enjoy your delicious homemade Thai Green Curry Soup with Chicken and Eggplant! Adjust the spiciness level by adding more or fewer green Thai chilies according to your preference.

Chinese Hot and Spicy Soup with Pork and Vegetables

Ingredients:

- 8 cups chicken or pork broth
- 1/2 pound pork tenderloin or pork shoulder, thinly sliced
- 1 tablespoon vegetable oil
- 2 cloves garlic, minced
- 1-inch piece ginger, grated
- 1 red bell pepper, thinly sliced
- 1 cup sliced mushrooms (shiitake, button, or any variety)
- 1 cup shredded cabbage
- 1/2 cup sliced bamboo shoots
- 1/4 cup soy sauce
- 2 tablespoons rice vinegar
- 1 tablespoon chili paste or chili oil (adjust to taste)
- 1 tablespoon cornstarch, dissolved in 2 tablespoons water
- 2 green onions, thinly sliced
- Salt and pepper, to taste
- Cooked rice or noodles, for serving
- Fresh cilantro leaves, for garnish (optional)

Instructions:

1. Prepare the Pork:
    - In a skillet or wok, heat the vegetable oil over medium-high heat. Add the thinly sliced pork and stir-fry until browned and cooked through, about 3-4 minutes. Remove the pork from the skillet and set aside.
2. Make the Soup Base:
    - In a large pot, bring the chicken or pork broth to a simmer over medium heat.
    - Add the minced garlic and grated ginger to the pot. Let it simmer for a few minutes to infuse the broth with flavor.
3. Add Vegetables and Seasonings:
    - Add the thinly sliced red bell pepper, sliced mushrooms, shredded cabbage, and sliced bamboo shoots to the pot.
    - Stir in the soy sauce, rice vinegar, and chili paste or chili oil. Taste the soup and adjust the seasoning with salt and pepper as needed.
4. Thicken the Soup:
    - Slowly pour the cornstarch mixture into the simmering soup while stirring continuously. This will help thicken the soup slightly.
    - Let the soup simmer for another 5-7 minutes, or until the vegetables are tender and the soup has thickened slightly.

5. Add Pork and Green Onions:
    - Add the cooked pork slices back into the pot.
    - Stir in the thinly sliced green onions.
6. Serve:
    - Ladle the hot Chinese Hot and Spicy Soup with Pork and Vegetables into serving bowls.
    - Garnish each bowl with fresh cilantro leaves, if desired.
    - Serve the soup hot, accompanied by cooked rice or noodles on the side.

Enjoy your delicious homemade Chinese Hot and Spicy Soup with Pork and Vegetables! Adjust the spiciness level by adding more or less chili paste or chili oil according to your preference.

Korean Tteokguk Soup with Rice Cakes and Beef

Ingredients:

- 8 cups beef broth or anchovy broth
- 1/2 pound beef (flank steak or sirloin), thinly sliced
- 1 tablespoon soy sauce
- 1 tablespoon sesame oil
- 1 tablespoon minced garlic
- Salt and pepper, to taste
- 1 package (about 14 ounces) sliced Korean rice cakes (tteok)
- 4 green onions, thinly sliced
- 2 eggs
- Toasted sesame seeds, for garnish
- Kimchi, for serving (optional)

Instructions:

1. Prepare the Beef:
    - In a bowl, combine the thinly sliced beef with soy sauce, sesame oil, minced garlic, salt, and pepper. Mix well and set aside to marinate while you prepare the other ingredients.
2. Prepare the Soup Base:
    - In a large pot, bring the beef broth to a boil over medium-high heat.
3. Add the Rice Cakes:
    - Once the broth is boiling, add the sliced rice cakes to the pot. Stir gently to prevent sticking.
    - Reduce the heat to medium and let the rice cakes cook for about 5-7 minutes, or until they are tender and chewy.
4. Cook the Beef:
    - While the rice cakes are cooking, add the marinated beef to the pot. Stir gently to separate the beef slices and cook until they are no longer pink, about 2-3 minutes.
5. Season and Garnish:
    - Season the soup with salt and pepper to taste.
    - Stir in most of the thinly sliced green onions, reserving some for garnish.
    - Sprinkle toasted sesame seeds over the soup.
6. Add Eggs:

- Crack the eggs into the soup, one at a time, making sure they are evenly distributed.
- Let the eggs cook for about 2-3 minutes until the whites are set but the yolks are still runny.

7. Serve:
    - Ladle the hot Korean Tteokguk Soup with Rice Cakes and Beef into serving bowls.
    - Garnish each bowl with the remaining thinly sliced green onions.
    - Serve the soup hot, with kimchi on the side if desired.

Enjoy your delicious homemade Korean Tteokguk Soup with Rice Cakes and Beef! It's a comforting and flavorful dish that's perfect for any occasion.

Japanese Tonjiru Soup with Pork and Vegetables

Ingredients:

- 8 cups dashi broth (can substitute with chicken or vegetable broth)
- 1/2 pound pork belly or pork shoulder, thinly sliced
- 1 tablespoon vegetable oil
- 1 onion, thinly sliced
- 2 carrots, sliced
- 1 daikon radish, peeled and sliced
- 1 potato, peeled and diced
- 1/2 cup sliced shiitake mushrooms
- 1/2 cup sliced konjac noodles (optional)
- 1/4 cup miso paste (white or red)
- 2 tablespoons soy sauce
- 1 tablespoon mirin (Japanese sweet rice wine)
- 1 tablespoon sake (Japanese rice wine) or dry sherry
- 2 green onions, thinly sliced
- Salt and pepper, to taste
- Cooked rice, for serving
- Toasted sesame seeds, for garnish
- Shichimi togarashi (Japanese seven spice), for garnish (optional)

Instructions:

1. Prepare the Pork:
    - In a large pot, heat the vegetable oil over medium heat. Add the thinly sliced pork belly or pork shoulder and cook until browned.
2. Add Vegetables:
    - Add the thinly sliced onion, sliced carrots, sliced daikon radish, diced potato, and sliced shiitake mushrooms to the pot. Stir to combine.
3. Make the Soup Base:
    - Pour in the dashi broth (or chicken/vegetable broth) into the pot. Bring the mixture to a simmer over medium heat.
4. Add Seasonings:
    - In a small bowl, mix the miso paste with a ladleful of hot broth until smooth. Add the miso mixture back into the pot.
    - Stir in the soy sauce, mirin, and sake. Taste the soup and adjust the seasoning with salt and pepper as needed.
5. Simmer:
    - Let the soup simmer gently for about 15-20 minutes, or until the vegetables are tender and the flavors have melded together.

6. Add Konjac Noodles (Optional):
   - If using konjac noodles, add them to the pot during the last few minutes of cooking. Allow them to heat through.
7. Serve:
   - Ladle the hot Tonjiru Soup with Pork and Vegetables into serving bowls.
   - Garnish each bowl with thinly sliced green onions, toasted sesame seeds, and a sprinkle of shichimi togarashi, if desired.
   - Serve the soup hot, accompanied by cooked rice on the side.

Enjoy your delicious homemade Japanese Tonjiru Soup with Pork and Vegetables! It's a comforting and satisfying dish that's perfect for cold days.

Thai Tom Yum Talay Soup with Mixed Seafood and Lemongrass

Ingredients:

- 4 cups seafood broth
- 1 stalk lemongrass, bruised and chopped
- 4 kaffir lime leaves, torn
- 2 Thai bird's eye chilies, sliced (adjust to taste)
- 2 tablespoons galangal, sliced
- 1 tablespoon fish sauce
- 1 tablespoon lime juice
- 1 teaspoon sugar
- 200g mixed seafood (shrimp, squid, mussels)
- 1 tomato, sliced
- 1 small onion, sliced
- 1 cup straw mushrooms
- Fresh cilantro leaves, for garnish
- Thai basil leaves, for garnish

Instructions:

1. Prepare the Broth:
   - In a pot, bring the seafood broth to a boil over medium heat.
   - Add the lemongrass, kaffir lime leaves, Thai bird's eye chilies, and galangal to the pot. Let it simmer for about 5-10 minutes to infuse the flavors.
2. Add Seasonings:
   - Stir in the fish sauce, lime juice, and sugar. Taste the broth and adjust the seasoning as needed.
3. Cook the Seafood:
   - Add the mixed seafood (shrimp, squid, mussels) to the pot. Let it simmer until the seafood is cooked through.
4. Add Vegetables:
   - Add the sliced tomato, onion, and straw mushrooms to the pot. Let them cook for a few more minutes until softened.
5. Serve:
   - Ladle the hot Tom Yum Talay Soup into serving bowls.
   - Garnish each bowl with fresh cilantro leaves and Thai basil leaves.
   - Serve the soup hot as a comforting and flavorful meal.

Enjoy your delicious homemade Thai Tom Yum Talay Soup with Mixed Seafood and Lemongrass! Adjust the spiciness level by adding more or fewer Thai bird's eye chilies according to your taste preferences.

Chinese Egg Flower Soup with Corn and Chicken

Ingredients:

- 6 cups chicken broth
- 1 cup cooked chicken breast, shredded
- 1 cup canned corn kernels, drained
- 2 eggs
- 2 tablespoons cornstarch
- 2 tablespoons water
- 2 green onions, thinly sliced
- Salt and pepper, to taste
- Sesame oil, for drizzling (optional)
- Fresh cilantro leaves, for garnish (optional)

Instructions:

1. Prepare the Soup Base:
    - In a pot, bring the chicken broth to a gentle simmer over medium heat.
2. Add Chicken and Corn:
    - Add the shredded cooked chicken breast and canned corn kernels to the pot. Let them heat through for a few minutes.
3. Thicken the Soup:
    - In a small bowl, mix the cornstarch with water to create a slurry. Slowly pour the cornstarch slurry into the simmering soup while stirring continuously. This will help thicken the soup slightly.
4. Create Egg Flowers:
    - In a separate bowl, beat the eggs until well mixed. Slowly pour the beaten eggs into the simmering soup in a thin stream while stirring the soup gently with a fork or chopsticks. This will create delicate egg "flowers" in the soup.
5. Season and Garnish:
    - Season the soup with salt and pepper to taste. Stir in thinly sliced green onions.
    - Drizzle a few drops of sesame oil over the soup for extra flavor, if desired.
    - Garnish each bowl with fresh cilantro leaves for a burst of freshness.
6. Serve:
    - Ladle the hot Chinese Egg Flower Soup with Corn and Chicken into serving bowls.
    - Serve the soup hot as a comforting and nourishing meal.

Enjoy your delicious homemade Chinese Egg Flower Soup with Corn and Chicken! It's a light yet sat sfying dish that's perfect for any occasion.

Vietnamese Bun Mang Vit Soup with Duck and Bamboo Shoots

Ingredients:

- 1 whole duck (about 3-4 pounds), cleaned and cut into pieces
- 8 cups water
- 2 stalks lemongrass, bruised
- 1 onion, peeled and halved
- 1-inch piece ginger, sliced
- 3 star anise
- 2 cinnamon sticks
- 1 tablespoon sugar
- 1 tablespoon salt
- 1 pound fresh bamboo shoots, peeled and sliced
- 1 package (about 8 ounces) dried rice vermicelli noodles (bun)
- 1/2 cup chopped cilantro
- 1/2 cup chopped green onions
- Lime wedges, for serving
- Thai basil leaves, for serving
- Bean sprouts, for serving
- Sliced chili peppers, for serving (optional)

Instructions:

1. Prepare the Duck Broth:
    - In a large pot, bring the water to a boil over high heat. Add the duck pieces, lemongrass stalks, halved onion, sliced ginger, star anise, cinnamon sticks, sugar, and salt to the pot.
    - Reduce the heat to low and let the broth simmer gently for about 2-3 hours, skimming off any impurities that rise to the surface.
2. Cook the Bamboo Shoots:
    - In a separate pot, bring water to a boil. Add the sliced bamboo shoots and blanch them for about 5-7 minutes. Drain and set aside.
3. Prepare the Rice Vermicelli Noodles:
    - Cook the dried rice vermicelli noodles according to the package instructions. Drain and set aside.
4. Serve:
    - To serve, divide the cooked rice vermicelli noodles among serving bowls.
    - Top the noodles with pieces of cooked duck, blanched bamboo shoots, chopped cilantro, and chopped green onions.
    - Ladle the hot duck broth over the noodles and garnish each bowl with lime wedges, Thai basil leaves, bean sprouts, and sliced chili peppers, if desired.

5. Enjoy:
    - Serve the Vietnamese Bun Mang Vit Soup hot and enjoy the rich flavors and comforting warmth.

This Vietnamese Bun Mang Vit Soup with Duck and Bamboo Shoots is a delicious and satisfying meal that's sure to impress. Enjoy it with family and friends for a delightful culinary experience!

Korean Samgyetang Soup with Ginseng and Chicken

Ingredients:

- 1 whole young chicken (about 3-4 pounds), cleaned and cavity emptied
- 10 cups water
- 4 garlic cloves, peeled
- 6 dried jujubes (Korean red dates)
- 4 ginseng roots, washed and soaked in water for 30 minutes
- 1 cup sweet rice (glutinous rice), soaked in water for 1 hour
- Salt, to taste
- Chopped green onions, for garnish
- Toasted sesame seeds, for garnish

Instructions:

1. Prepare the Chicken:
    - Rinse the chicken under cold water and pat it dry with paper towels. Stuff the cavity of the chicken with soaked sweet rice, garlic cloves, dried jujubes, and soaked ginseng roots.
2. Cook the Soup:
    - In a large pot, bring the water to a boil over high heat. Add the stuffed chicken to the pot.
    - Reduce the heat to low and let the soup simmer gently, partially covered, for about 1.5 to 2 hours, or until the chicken is tender and the rice inside the cavity is cooked through.
3. Season and Serve:
    - Once the chicken is cooked, season the soup with salt to taste.
    - Ladle the hot Samgyetang Soup into serving bowls, making sure to include a portion of the chicken, rice, and ginseng in each bowl.
    - Garnish each bowl with chopped green onions and toasted sesame seeds for added flavor and presentation.
4. Enjoy:
    - Serve the Korean Samgyetang Soup hot as a nourishing and comforting meal, especially during cold weather or when feeling under the weather.

This Korean Samgyetang Soup with Ginseng and Chicken is a traditional dish known for its rejuvenating properties and rich flavors. Enjoy it as a nutritious meal that's both satisfying and revitalizing!

Japanese Ochazuke Soup with Grilled Salmon and Green Tea

Ingredients:

- 2 cups cooked Japanese rice
- 2 cups hot green tea (sencha or genmaicha)
- 2 grilled salmon fillets, flaked
- 2 tablespoons nori seaweed, thinly sliced
- 2 green onions, thinly sliced
- Soy sauce, to taste
- Wasabi paste, to taste (optional)
- Toasted sesame seeds, for garnish
- Pickled plum (umeboshi), for garnish (optional)

Instructions:

1. Prepare the Green Tea:
    - Brew the green tea using hot water according to the package instructions. Set aside.
2. Assemble the Ochazuke:
    - Divide the cooked Japanese rice evenly into serving bowls.
    - Place the grilled salmon fillets on top of the rice in each bowl.
3. Pour the Green Tea:
    - Pour the hot green tea over the rice and salmon in each bowl, covering them completely.
4. Add Toppings:
    - Sprinkle thinly sliced nori seaweed and green onions over the top of each bowl.
    - Optionally, add a small amount of wasabi paste for extra flavor.
5. Season and Garnish:
    - Drizzle soy sauce over each bowl to taste.
    - Sprinkle toasted sesame seeds over the top for added texture and flavor.
    - Optionally, garnish each bowl with a pickled plum (umeboshi) for a tangy contrast.
6. Serve:
    - Serve the Japanese Ochazuke Soup with Grilled Salmon and Green Tea immediately while still hot.

This Ochazuke Soup with Grilled Salmon and Green Tea is a delightful and nourishing dish that's both simple to make and full of comforting flavors. Enjoy it as a light meal or snack any time of the day!

Thai Gaeng Jued Woon Sen Soup with Glass Noodles and Tofu

Ingredients:

- 4 cups vegetable broth
- 100g dried glass noodles (woon sen)
- 200g firm tofu, cubed
- 1 cup sliced mushrooms (such as shiitake or button mushrooms)
- 1 carrot, thinly sliced
- 1 cup baby spinach leaves
- 2 tablespoons soy sauce
- 1 tablespoon rice vinegar
- 1 tablespoon sugar
- 2 cloves garlic, minced
- 1 tablespoon grated ginger
- 2 green onions, thinly sliced
- Fresh cilantro leaves, for garnish
- Lime wedges, for serving
- Thai chili peppers, thinly sliced (optional, for garnish)

Instructions:

1. Prepare the Glass Noodles:
    - Place the dried glass noodles in a bowl and cover them with hot water. Let them soak for about 10 minutes, or until they are soft. Drain and set aside.
2. Cook the Tofu:
    - In a large pot, heat a little bit of oil over medium heat. Add the cubed tofu and cook until it is golden brown on all sides. Remove the tofu from the pot and set it aside.
3. Make the Soup Base:
    - In the same pot, add minced garlic and grated ginger. Sauté for a minute until fragrant.
    - Pour in the vegetable broth and bring it to a simmer over medium heat.
4. Add Vegetables:
    - Add sliced mushrooms and thinly sliced carrots to the pot. Let them cook for a few minutes until slightly softened.
5. Season the Soup:
    - Stir in soy sauce, rice vinegar, and sugar. Taste the soup and adjust the seasoning as needed.
6. Add Glass Noodles and Tofu:
    - Add the soaked glass noodles and cooked tofu to the pot. Let them simmer for a couple of minutes until heated through.
7. Finish and Serve:

- Add baby spinach leaves and thinly sliced green onions to the pot. Let the spinach wilt slightly.
- Ladle the hot Gaeng Jued Woon Sen Soup into serving bowls.
- Garnish each bowl with fresh cilantro leaves and serve with lime wedges and Thai chili peppers on the side, if desired.

Enjoy your delicious homemade Thai Gaeng Jued Woon Sen Soup with Glass Noodles and Tofu! It's a light and satisfying dish that's bursting with flavor and texture.

Chinese Seafood Congee with Rice and Vegetables

Ingredients:

- 1 cup jasmine rice, rinsed
- 8 cups water or seafood broth
- 200g mixed seafood (shrimp, squid, mussels), cleaned and chopped
- 1 carrot, diced
- 1 small zucchini, diced
- 1 cup spinach leaves, chopped
- 2 green onions, thinly sliced
- 2 cloves garlic, minced
- 1-inch piece ginger, grated
- 2 tablespoons soy sauce
- 1 tablespoon rice vinegar
- Salt and pepper, to taste
- Sesame oil, for drizzling (optional)
- Toasted sesame seeds, for garnish
- Fresh cilantro leaves, for garnish

Instructions:

1. Cook the Congee:
    - In a large pot, bring the water or seafood broth to a boil over high heat. Add the rinsed jasmine rice to the pot and reduce the heat to medium-low. Let the rice simmer, stirring occasionally, until it becomes thick and creamy, about 30-40 minutes.
2. Prepare the Seafood and Vegetables:
    - While the congee is cooking, prepare the seafood and vegetables. Clean and chop the mixed seafood (shrimp, squid, mussels) and set aside. Dice the carrot and zucchini, chop the spinach leaves, and thinly slice the green onions.
3. Add Seafood and Vegetables:
    - Once the congee is thick and creamy, add the chopped seafood, diced carrot, and diced zucchini to the pot. Let them cook for about 5-7 minutes, or until the seafood is cooked through and the vegetables are tender.
4. Season the Congee:
    - Stir in minced garlic, grated ginger, soy sauce, and rice vinegar. Season with salt and pepper to taste. Adjust the seasoning as needed.
5. Serve:
    - Ladle the hot Seafood Congee with Rice and Vegetables into serving bowls.
    - Drizzle with a little sesame oil for extra flavor, if desired.

- Garnish each bowl with thinly sliced green onions, toasted sesame seeds, and fresh cilantro leaves.

Enjoy your delicious homemade Chinese Seafood Congee with Rice and Vegetables! It's a hearty and satisfying dish that's full of flavor and nutrients.

Korean Sundubu Jjigae Soup with Soft Tofu and Kimchi

Ingredients:

- 1 block (about 14 ounces) soft tofu (sundubu), cut into cubes
- 1 cup kimchi, chopped
- 1/2 cup kimchi juice (from the jar)
- 2 cups vegetable or seafood broth
- 1/2 cup water
- 1/2 onion, thinly sliced
- 2 cloves garlic, minced
- 2 green onions, chopped
- 1 tablespoon gochugaru (Korean red pepper flakes)
- 1 tablespoon gochujang (Korean red pepper paste)
- 1 tablespoon soy sauce
- 1 teaspoon sesame oil
- 1 teaspoon sugar
- 1 tablespoon vegetable oil
- Salt and pepper, to taste
- 1 egg (optional)
- Fresh cilantro or green onions, for garnish

Instructions:

1. Prepare the Ingredients:
   - Cut the soft tofu into cubes and chop the kimchi.
   - Thinly slice the onion, mince the garlic, and chop the green onions.
2. Make the Soup Base:
   - In a large pot, heat the vegetable oil over medium heat. Add the sliced onion and minced garlic. Cook until softened and fragrant.
   - Add the chopped kimchi to the pot along with the kimchi juice. Cook for a few minutes to allow the flavors to meld.
3. Add Seasonings:
   - Stir in the gochugaru (Korean red pepper flakes), gochujang (Korean red pepper paste), soy sauce, sesame oil, and sugar. Mix well to combine.
4. Add Broth and Water:
   - Pour in the vegetable or seafood broth and water. Bring the mixture to a simmer.
5. Add Tofu and Simmer:
   - Gently add the cubed soft tofu to the pot. Let the soup simmer for about 5-7 minutes to allow the flavors to blend and the tofu to heat through.
6. Adjust Seasoning:

- Taste the soup and adjust the seasoning with salt and pepper as needed. Add more gochugaru or gochujang for extra spice, if desired.
7. Optional: Add Egg:
    - If using, crack an egg into the simmering soup. Let it cook until the whites are set but the yolk is still runny.
8. Serve:
    - Ladle the hot Sundubu Jjigae Soup into serving bowls.
    - Garnish each bowl with chopped green onions or fresh cilantro.

Enjoy your delicious homemade Korean Sundubu Jjigae Soup with Soft Tofu and Kimchi! It's best served piping hot and enjoyed with a bowl of steamed rice.

Japanese Chawanmushi Soup with Steamed Egg and Shrimp

Ingredients:

- 2 cups dashi broth (Japanese soup stock)
- 3 large eggs
- 1/2 cup cooked shrimp, peeled and deveined
- 2 fresh shiitake mushrooms, sliced
- 2 tablespoons soy sauce
- 1 tablespoon mirin (Japanese sweet rice wine)
- 1/2 teaspoon salt
- 1/2 teaspoon sugar
- 1 green onion, thinly sliced (for garnish)
- Mitsuba leaves or cilantro, for garnish (optional)

Instructions:

1. Prepare the Dashi Broth:
    - In a saucepan, bring the dashi broth to a gentle simmer over medium heat. Keep it warm.
2. Prepare the Steamed Egg Mixture:
    - In a mixing bowl, lightly beat the eggs. Be careful not to create too many bubbles.
    - Gradually pour the warm dashi broth into the beaten eggs while stirring gently. Strain the mixture through a fine sieve to remove any lumps.
3. Season the Mixture:
    - Stir in soy sauce, mirin, salt, and sugar until well combined.
4. Assemble the Chawanmushi:
    - Divide the cooked shrimp and sliced shiitake mushrooms evenly among small teacups or ramekins.
    - Pour the steamed egg mixture over the shrimp and mushrooms, filling each cup almost to the top.
5. Steam the Chawanmushi:
    - Place the teacups or ramekins in a steamer basket or on a rack in a large pot. Cover with a lid.
    - Steam the Chawanmushi over medium-low heat for about 15-20 minutes, or until the egg mixture is set but still slightly jiggly in the center.
6. Serve:
    - Carefully remove the Chawanmushi from the steamer. Garnish each cup with thinly sliced green onions and mitsuba leaves or cilantro, if using.
    - Serve the Chawanmushi hot as an appetizer or light meal.

Enjoy your delicious homemade Japanese Chawanmushi Soup with Steamed Egg and Shrimp! It's a delightful combination of silky steamed egg custard, tender shrimp, and savory mushrooms, all infused with the delicate flavors of dashi broth.

Thai Spicy Lemongrass Soup with Chicken and Rice Noodles

Ingredients:

- 6 cups chicken broth
- 200g rice noodles
- 2 boneless, skinless chicken breasts, thinly sliced
- 2 stalks lemongrass, bruised and sliced into segments
- 3 kaffir lime leaves, torn
- 3-4 slices galangal
- 2-3 Thai bird's eye chilies, thinly sliced (adjust to taste)
- 1 tomato, cut into wedges
- 1 onion, thinly sliced
- 200g mushrooms (such as straw mushrooms or button mushrooms), sliced
- 2 tablespoons fish sauce
- 2 tablespoons lime juice
- 1 tablespoon sugar
- Salt, to taste
- Fresh cilantro leaves, for garnish
- Thai basil leaves, for garnish
- Sliced red chili peppers, for garnish (optional)

Instructions:

1. Prepare the Rice Noodles:
    - Cook the rice noodles according to the package instructions. Drain and set aside.
2. Make the Soup Base:
    - In a large pot, bring the chicken broth to a gentle simmer over medium heat.
    - Add the sliced lemongrass, torn kaffir lime leaves, galangal slices, and Thai bird's eye chilies to the pot. Let it simmer for about 5-10 minutes to infuse the flavors.
3. Add Chicken and Vegetables:
    - Add the thinly sliced chicken breasts, tomato wedges, thinly sliced onion, and sliced mushrooms to the pot. Let them cook for a few minutes until the chicken is cooked through and the vegetables are tender.
4. Season the Soup:
    - Stir in fish sauce, lime juice, and sugar. Taste the soup and adjust the seasoning with salt if needed. The soup should be savory, tangy, and slightly sweet.
5. Assemble the Soup:
    - Divide the cooked rice noodles among serving bowls.
    - Ladle the hot Spicy Lemongrass Soup with Chicken and Vegetables over the rice noodles.
6. Garnish and Serve:

- Garnish each bowl with fresh cilantro leaves and Thai basil leaves.
- Optionally, add sliced red chili peppers for extra heat, if desired.

7. Enjoy:
    - Serve the Thai Spicy Lemongrass Soup hot as a comforting and flavorful meal.

Enjoy your delicious homemade Thai Spicy Lemongrass Soup with Chicken and Rice Noodles! It's a refreshing and satisfying dish that's perfect for any occasion. Adjust the spiciness level by adding more or fewer Thai bird's eye chilies according to your taste preferences.

Chinese Winter Melon Soup with Pork and Shiitake Mushrooms

Ingredients:

- 500g winter melon, peeled and cut into bite-sized pieces
- 200g pork loin or pork belly, thinly sliced
- 4-5 dried shiitake mushrooms, soaked in hot water until softened
- 1 liter chicken or pork broth
- 2 slices ginger
- 2 cloves garlic, minced
- 2 green onions, chopped
- 1 tablespoon Shaoxing wine (Chinese cooking wine)
- 1 tablespoon soy sauce
- Salt and white pepper, to taste
- 1 tablespoon vegetable oil
- Fresh cilantro leaves, for garnish (optional)

Instructions:

1. Prepare the Ingredients:
    - Peel the winter melon and cut it into bite-sized pieces. Soak the dried shiitake mushrooms in hot water until softened, then slice them thinly. Thinly slice the pork loin or pork belly.
2. Cook the Pork:
    - Heat vegetable oil in a pot over medium heat. Add the minced garlic and ginger slices, and sauté until fragrant.
    - Add the sliced pork and cook until it is lightly browned on all sides.
3. Add Broth and Seasonings:
    - Pour in the chicken or pork broth and Shaoxing wine. Bring the mixture to a boil, then reduce the heat to low and let it simmer for about 10 minutes.
4. Add Winter Melon and Shiitake Mushrooms:
    - Add the winter melon pieces and sliced shiitake mushrooms to the pot. Simmer for another 15-20 minutes, or until the winter melon is tender.
5. Season the Soup:
    - Stir in soy sauce, chopped green onions, salt, and white pepper to taste. Adjust the seasoning as needed.
6. Serve:
    - Ladle the hot Winter Melon Soup with Pork and Shiitake Mushrooms into serving bowls.
    - Garnish each bowl with fresh cilantro leaves, if desired.

Enjoy your delicious homemade Chinese Winter Melon Soup with Pork and Shiitake Mushrooms! It's a comforting and nutritious dish that's perfect for warming up during the colder months.

Vietnamese Bun Rieu Cua Soup with Crab and Tomato Broth

Ingredients:

For the broth:

- 500g crab meat (fresh or canned)
- 1 can (400g) diced tomatoes
- 1 onion, chopped
- 3 cloves garlic, minced
- 1 tablespoon shrimp paste (mam ruoc)
- 1 tablespoon fish sauce
- 1 tablespoon sugar
- 1 teaspoon annatto seeds (optional, for color)
- 8 cups water or seafood broth

For the soup:

- 200g firm tofu, diced
- 200g pork, minced
- 200g shrimp, peeled and deveined
- 2 eggs
- 200g fresh crab meat (optional)
- 100g dried shrimp (optional)
- 200g rice vermicelli noodles (bun)
- Green onions, chopped (for garnish)
- Vietnamese coriander (rau ram) or cilantro, chopped (for garnish)
- Lime wedges (for serving)
- Bean sprouts (for serving)
- Thai basil leaves (for serving)
- Sliced chili peppers (for serving)

Instructions:

1. Prepare the Broth:
    - In a large pot, heat some oil over medium heat. Add chopped onions and minced garlic, and sauté until fragrant.
    - Add the crab meat (fresh or canned) to the pot and cook for a few minutes.
    - Stir in diced tomatoes, shrimp paste, fish sauce, sugar, and annatto seeds (if using). Cook for another 5 minutes.

- Pour in water or seafood broth and bring the mixture to a boil. Reduce the heat and let it simmer for about 30 minutes to allow the flavors to meld.
2. Prepare the Soup Base:
    - While the broth is simmering, prepare the soup base. In a bowl, mix minced pork with diced tofu, and season with salt and pepper. Form small meatballs from the mixture.
    - In another bowl, beat the eggs and set aside.
3. Add Protein and Noodles:
    - Once the broth is ready, add the meatballs, peeled and deveined shrimp, fresh crab meat (if using), and dried shrimp (if using) to the pot. Let them cook for about 5-7 minutes until the meatballs are cooked through and the shrimp are pink.
    - Meanwhile, cook the rice vermicelli noodles according to the package instructions. Drain and set aside.
4. Finish and Serve:
    - Slowly pour the beaten eggs into the simmering broth while stirring gently to create egg ribbons.
    - To serve, divide the cooked rice vermicelli noodles among serving bowls. Ladle the hot Bun Rieu Cua Soup over the noodles.
    - Garnish each bowl with chopped green onions and Vietnamese coriander or cilantro.
    - Serve with lime wedges, bean sprouts, Thai basil leaves, and sliced chili peppers on the side for customization.

Enjoy your delicious homemade Vietnamese Bun Rieu Cua Soup with Crab and Tomato Broth! It's a comforting and hearty dish that's perfect for any occasion.

Korean Yukgaejang Soup with Spicy Beef and Vegetables

Ingredients:

- 400g beef brisket or flank steak, thinly sliced
- 1 onion, thinly sliced
- 3 cloves garlic, minced
- 2 green onions, chopped
- 1/2 cup fernbrake (gosari), soaked in hot water until softened
- 1/2 cup sliced oyster mushrooms
- 1/2 cup sliced shiitake mushrooms
- 1/2 cup julienned carrots
- 1/2 cup julienned zucchini
- 1/2 cup chopped leek
- 6 cups beef broth
- 2 tablespoons soy sauce
- 1 tablespoon gochugaru (Korean red pepper flakes)
- 1 tablespoon gochujang (Korean red pepper paste)
- 1 tablespoon sesame oil
- 1 tablespoon fish sauce
- 1 teaspoon ground black pepper
- Salt, to taste
- Cooked white rice, for serving
- Korean radish (mu) and kimchi, for serving (optional)
- Toasted sesame seeds, for garnish
- Sliced green onions, for garnish

Instructions:

1. Prepare the Beef and Vegetables:
    - In a large pot, heat some vegetable oil over medium-high heat. Add the thinly sliced beef and minced garlic. Cook until the beef is browned.
2. Add Broth and Seasonings:
    - Pour in the beef broth and bring it to a boil. Add sliced onions, chopped green onions, fernbrake (gosari), oyster mushrooms, shiitake mushrooms, carrots, zucchini, and leek.
    - Stir in soy sauce, gochugaru (Korean red pepper flakes), gochujang (Korean red pepper paste), sesame oil, fish sauce, ground black pepper, and salt to taste. Mix well to combine.
3. Simmer the Soup:

- Reduce the heat to low and let the soup simmer for about 1 to 1.5 hours, or until the beef is tender and the vegetables are cooked through. Skim off any foam or impurities that rise to the surface.
4. Serve:
    - Ladle the hot Yukgaejang Soup into serving bowls. Garnish each bowl with toasted sesame seeds and sliced green onions.
    - Serve the soup hot with cooked white rice on the side. You can also serve it with Korean radish (mu) and kimchi for extra flavor and texture.

Enjoy your delicious homemade Korean Yukgaejang Soup with Spicy Beef and Vegetables! It's a satisfying and comforting dish that's sure to warm you up from the inside out.

Japanese Nabeyaki Udon Soup with Tempura and Egg

Ingredients:

For the soup:

- 4 cups dashi stock (Japanese soup stock)
- 1/4 cup soy sauce
- 2 tablespoons mirin (Japanese sweet rice wine)
- 2 tablespoons sake (Japanese rice wine)
- 2 tablespoons sugar
- 1 tablespoon miso paste
- 200g udon noodles
- 1 cup sliced mushrooms (shiitake, shimeji, or enoki)
- 1 cup sliced carrots
- 1 cup sliced bamboo shoots
- 1 cup spinach leaves
- 2 green onions, sliced
- Salt, to taste

For the tempura:

- Assorted vegetables (such as sweet potato, onion, bell pepper, and eggplant)
- 1 cup all-purpose flour
- 1 cup ice-cold water
- Vegetable oil, for frying

For the toppings:

- 4 eggs
- Toasted sesame seeds, for garnish
- Nori (seaweed), for garnish
- Shichimi togarashi (Japanese seven spice), for garnish (optional)

Instructions:

1. Prepare the Soup Base:

- In a large pot, combine dashi stock, soy sauce, mirin, sake, sugar, and miso paste. Bring the mixture to a gentle simmer over medium heat, stirring until the miso paste is fully dissolved.
    - Add sliced mushrooms, carrots, and bamboo shoots to the pot. Let them simmer for a few minutes until slightly tender.
2. Cook the Udon Noodles:
    - Cook the udon noodles according to the package instructions. Drain and set aside.
3. Prepare the Tempura:
    - Heat vegetable oil in a deep fryer or large pot to 350°F (180°C).
    - In a mixing bowl, combine all-purpose flour and ice-cold water to make the tempura batter. It should have a thin consistency.
    - Dip assorted vegetables into the tempura batter, coating them evenly.
    - Fry the battered vegetables in the hot oil until golden brown and crispy. Remove them from the oil and drain on a paper towel-lined plate.
4. Add Spinach and Green Onions:
    - Add spinach leaves and sliced green onions to the soup pot. Let the spinach wilt slightly.
    - Season the soup with salt to taste.
5. Prepare the Toppings:
    - In a separate pot of simmering water, poach eggs until the whites are set but the yolks are still runny.
6. Assemble the Nabeyaki Udon:
    - Divide cooked udon noodles among individual serving bowls.
    - Ladle the hot soup over the noodles, making sure to distribute the vegetables evenly.
    - Top each bowl with a poached egg and assorted tempura vegetables.
7. Garnish and Serve:
    - Garnish each bowl with toasted sesame seeds, nori strips, and shichimi togarashi (if using).
    - Serve the Nabeyaki Udon Soup with Tempura and Egg hot, with additional soy sauce or chili oil on the side for extra flavor, if desired.

Enjoy your delicious homemade Japanese Nabeyaki Udon Soup with Tempura and Egg! It's a delightful combination of savory broth, tender noodles, crispy tempura, and creamy poached egg that's sure to satisfy your cravings.

Thai Pad Thai Soup with Shrimp and Rice Noodles

Ingredients:

For the soup:

- 200g rice noodles (pad Thai noodles)
- 1 tablespoon vegetable oil
- 2 cloves garlic, minced
- 1 shallot, finely chopped
- 1 red chili, thinly sliced (adjust to taste)
- 200g shrimp, peeled and deveined
- 4 cups chicken or vegetable broth
- 2 tablespoons tamarind paste
- 2 tablespoons fish sauce
- 1 tablespoon soy sauce
- 1 tablespoon brown sugar (or palm sugar)
- 1 cup bean sprouts
- 1/4 cup chopped peanuts, for garnish
- Lime wedges, for serving
- Fresh cilantro leaves, for garnish
- Sliced green onions, for garnish
- Thai basil leaves, for garnish
- Red pepper flakes or Sriracha sauce, for extra heat (optional)

Instructions:

1. Prepare the Rice Noodles:
    - Cook the rice noodles according to the package instructions until they are al dente. Drain and set aside.
2. Make the Soup Base:
    - In a large pot, heat vegetable oil over medium heat. Add minced garlic, chopped shallot, and sliced red chili. Sauté for a few minutes until fragrant.
    - Add peeled and deveined shrimp to the pot and cook until they turn pink and opaque, about 2-3 minutes.
3. Add Broth and Seasonings:
    - Pour chicken or vegetable broth into the pot. Stir in tamarind paste, fish sauce, soy sauce, and brown sugar (or palm sugar). Allow the soup to simmer for about 5 minutes to allow the flavors to meld.
4. Add Noodles and Bean Sprouts:

- Add cooked rice noodles to the pot along with bean sprouts. Let them cook for another 2-3 minutes until heated through.
5. Serve:
    - Ladle the hot Pad Thai Soup with Shrimp and Rice Noodles into serving bowls.
    - Garnish each bowl with chopped peanuts, fresh cilantro leaves, sliced green onions, and Thai basil leaves.
    - Serve the soup hot with lime wedges on the side for squeezing over the soup just before eating.
    - Optionally, add red pepper flakes or Sriracha sauce for extra heat, according to taste preferences.

Enjoy your delicious homemade Thai Pad Thai Soup with Shrimp and Rice Noodles! It's a comforting and satisfying dish packed with vibrant flavors and textures.

Chinese Chicken Corn Soup with Egg Ribbons and Vegetables

Ingredients:

- 4 cups chicken broth
- 1 cup cooked chicken breast, shredded
- 1 cup canned corn kernels, drained
- 1 carrot, julienned
- 1/2 cup frozen peas
- 2 eggs
- 2 tablespoons cornstarch
- 2 tablespoons water
- 1 tablespoon soy sauce
- 1 teaspoon sesame oil
- Salt and white pepper, to taste
- Green onions, chopped (for garnish)
- Fresh cilantro leaves (for garnish)

Instructions:

1. Prepare the Soup Base:
   - In a large pot, bring the chicken broth to a simmer over medium heat.
   - Add shredded chicken breast, canned corn kernels, julienned carrot, and frozen peas to the pot. Let them simmer for a few minutes until the vegetables are tender.
2. Create Egg Ribbons:
   - In a small bowl, beat the eggs. Slowly pour the beaten eggs into the simmering soup in a thin stream while stirring gently with chopsticks or a fork. This will create egg ribbons in the soup.
3. Thicken the Soup:
   - In another small bowl, mix cornstarch with water to create a slurry. Gradually pour the cornstarch slurry into the soup while stirring constantly. This will help thicken the soup slightly.
4. Season the Soup:
   - Stir in soy sauce and sesame oil. Season the soup with salt and white pepper to taste. Adjust the seasoning as needed.
5. Serve:
   - Ladle the hot Chicken Corn Soup into serving bowls.
   - Garnish each bowl with chopped green onions and fresh cilantro leaves for added flavor and freshness.

Enjoy your delicious homemade Chinese Chicken Corn Soup with Egg Ribbons and Vegetables! It's a comforting and nutritious dish that's perfect for any occasion.

Korean Janchi Guksu Soup with Hand-Cut Noodles and Beef

Ingredients:

For the broth:

- 8 cups beef or chicken broth
- 1 onion, quartered
- 2 cloves garlic, smashed
- 2 green onions, chopped
- 1-inch piece ginger, sliced
- 2 tablespoons soy sauce
- Salt, to taste

For the soup:

- 200g beef (such as sirloin or ribeye), thinly sliced
- 200g hand-cut noodles (or use store-bought dried noodles)
- 2 cups spinach, washed and trimmed
- 1 cup bean sprouts, washed
- 1 carrot, julienned
- 2 green onions, thinly sliced
- Toasted sesame seeds, for garnish
- Kimchi, for serving (optional)

Instructions:

1. Prepare the Broth:
    - In a large pot, combine beef or chicken broth, quartered onion, smashed garlic cloves, chopped green onions, sliced ginger, and soy sauce. Bring the mixture to a boil over high heat.
    - Reduce the heat to low and let the broth simmer for about 30 minutes to allow the flavors to meld. Season with salt to taste.
2. Prepare the Ingredients:
    - While the broth is simmering, prepare the remaining ingredients. Thinly slice the beef, wash and trim the spinach, wash the bean sprouts, julienne the carrot, and thinly slice the green onions.
3. Cook the Hand-Cut Noodles:
    - If using hand-cut noodles, cook them in a separate pot of boiling water according to the package instructions until they are al dente. Drain and set aside.

4. Assemble the Soup:
   - Once the broth is ready, add the thinly sliced beef to the pot. Let it cook for a few minutes until the beef is cooked through.
5. Add Vegetables and Noodles:
   - Add the cooked hand-cut noodles (or store-bought dried noodles), spinach, bean sprouts, julienned carrot, and thinly sliced green onions to the pot. Let them cook for another 2-3 minutes until the vegetables are tender and the noodles are heated through.
6. Serve:
   - Ladle the hot Janchi Guksu Soup into serving bowls.
   - Garnish each bowl with toasted sesame seeds for added flavor and texture.
   - Serve the soup hot with a side of kimchi, if desired, for extra flavor and spice.

Enjoy your delicious homemade Korean Janchi Guksu Soup with Hand-Cut Noodles and Beef! It's a comforting and satisfying dish that's perfect for any occasion.

Japanese Oden Soup with Various Fish Cakes and Daikon Radish

Ingredients:

For the broth:

- 8 cups dashi stock (Japanese soup stock)
- 1/4 cup soy sauce
- 2 tablespoons mirin (Japanese sweet rice wine)
- 1 tablespoon sake (Japanese rice wine)
- 1 tablespoon sugar
- 1/2 teaspoon salt

For the oden ingredients:

- Various fish cakes (such as kamaboko, chikuwa, hanpen, and atsuage)
- 1 daikon radish, peeled and cut into thick rounds
- 6 hard-boiled eggs, peeled
- 6 konnyaku (konjac) blocks, sliced into thick rounds
- 2-3 deep-fried tofu pouches (aburaage), cut in half diagonally
- 1/2 cabbage, cut into wedges
- 1 bunch spinach, washed and trimmed
- Green onions, chopped (for garnish)
- Shichimi togarashi (Japanese seven spice), for serving (optional)

Instructions:

1. Prepare the Broth:
    - In a large pot, combine dashi stock, soy sauce, mirin, sake, sugar, and salt. Bring the mixture to a boil over medium heat.
2. Prepare the Oden Ingredients:
    - While the broth is heating, prepare the oden ingredients. Cut the various fish cakes into bite-sized pieces.
    - Peel and cut the daikon radish into thick rounds. Score each round with a crisscross pattern to help them absorb the flavors of the broth.
    - Peel the hard-boiled eggs.
    - Slice the konnyaku blocks into thick rounds.
    - Cut the deep-fried tofu pouches in half diagonally.

- Cut the cabbage into wedges.
- Wash and trim the spinach.
3. Cook the Oden Ingredients:
    - Once the broth is boiling, add the daikon radish rounds to the pot. Let them simmer for about 10 minutes until they start to soften.
    - Add the fish cakes, hard-boiled eggs, konnyaku slices, deep-fried tofu pouches, and cabbage wedges to the pot. Let them simmer for another 10-15 minutes until all the ingredients are tender and infused with the flavors of the broth.
    - Add the spinach to the pot in the last few minutes of cooking, just until wilted.
4. Serve:
    - Ladle the hot Oden Soup with Various Fish Cakes and Daikon Radish into serving bowls.
    - Garnish each bowl with chopped green onions.
    - Serve the oden hot with a side of shichimi togarashi (Japanese seven spice) for extra flavor and spice, if desired.

Enjoy your delicious homemade Japanese Oden Soup with Various Fish Cakes and Daikon Radish! It's a comforting and satisfying dish that's perfect for warming up on chilly days.

Thai Peanut Noodle Soup with Chicken and Vegetables

Ingredients:

For the soup:

- 6 cups chicken broth
- 1 can (14 oz) coconut milk
- 1/2 cup creamy peanut butter
- 2 tablespoons red curry paste
- 2 tablespoons soy sauce
- 2 tablespoons brown sugar
- 2 cloves garlic, minced
- 1 tablespoon fresh ginger, grated
- 1 tablespoon lime juice
- Salt, to taste

For the soup toppings:

- 200g rice noodles
- 2 cups cooked chicken breast, shredded
- 1 cup broccoli florets
- 1 red bell pepper, thinly sliced
- 1 carrot, julienned
- 1 cup bean sprouts
- Fresh cilantro leaves, for garnish
- Crushed peanuts, for garnish
- Lime wedges, for serving

Instructions:

1. Prepare the Soup Base:
    - In a large pot, combine chicken broth, coconut milk, creamy peanut butter, red curry paste, soy sauce, brown sugar, minced garlic, grated ginger, and lime juice. Stir well to combine.
    - Bring the mixture to a simmer over medium heat, stirring occasionally to ensure that the peanut butter melts and blends evenly into the broth. Let it simmer for about 10 minutes to allow the flavors to meld. Season with salt to taste.
2. Cook the Rice Noodles:

- While the soup is simmering, cook the rice noodles according to the package instructions until they are al dente. Drain and set aside.
3. Add Chicken and Vegetables:
    - Once the soup base is ready, add shredded cooked chicken breast, broccoli florets, sliced red bell pepper, julienned carrot, and bean sprouts to the pot. Let them cook for about 5-7 minutes until the vegetables are tender-crisp and the chicken is heated through.
4. Assemble the Soup:
    - Divide the cooked rice noodles among serving bowls.
    - Ladle the hot Thai Peanut Noodle Soup with Chicken and Vegetables over the noodles, making sure to distribute the chicken and vegetables evenly.
5. Garnish and Serve:
    - Garnish each bowl with fresh cilantro leaves and crushed peanuts for added flavor and texture.
    - Serve the soup hot with lime wedges on the side for squeezing over the soup just before eating.

Enjoy your delicious homemade Thai Peanut Noodle Soup with Chicken and Vegetables! It's a comforting and satisfying dish that's bursting with Thai-inspired flavors.

Chinese Clear Vegetable Soup with Tofu and Chinese Greens

Ingredients:

- 6 cups vegetable broth or water
- 200g firm tofu, diced
- 2 cups Chinese greens (such as bok choy, gai lan, or choy sum), washed and chopped
- 1 carrot, thinly sliced
- 1 cup sliced mushrooms (such as shiitake, button, or oyster mushrooms)
- 2 cloves garlic, minced
- 1-inch piece ginger, thinly sliced
- 2 green onions, chopped
- 2 tablespoons soy sauce
- 1 tablespoon rice vinegar
- 1 tablespoon sesame oil
- Salt and white pepper, to taste
- Fresh cilantro leaves, for garnish

Instructions:

1. Prepare the Soup Base:
    - In a large pot, bring vegetable broth or water to a simmer over medium heat.
2. Add Aromatics and Seasonings:
    - Add minced garlic, thinly sliced ginger, and chopped green onions to the pot. Let them simmer in the broth for a few minutes to infuse the flavors.
    - Stir in soy sauce, rice vinegar, and sesame oil. Season the broth with salt and white pepper to taste.
3. Add Vegetables and Tofu:
    - Add diced tofu, thinly sliced carrots, sliced mushrooms, and chopped Chinese greens to the pot. Let them simmer for about 5-7 minutes until the vegetables are tender and the tofu is heated through.
4. Adjust Seasoning and Serve:
    - Taste the soup and adjust the seasoning if necessary, adding more soy sauce, rice vinegar, sesame oil, salt, or pepper to suit your taste preferences.
    - Ladle the hot Chinese Clear Vegetable Soup with Tofu and Chinese Greens into serving bowls.
5. Garnish and Serve:
    - Garnish each bowl with fresh cilantro leaves for added flavor and freshness.
    - Serve the soup hot as a light and nourishing meal or as a starter before the main course.

Enjoy your delicious homemade Chinese Clear Vegetable Soup with Tofu and Chinese Greens! It's a simple yet satisfying dish that's perfect for any occasion.

Vietnamese Bun Thang Soup with Chicken, Egg, and Vermicelli

Ingredients:

For the broth:

- 8 cups chicken broth
- 1 onion, peeled and halved
- 2-inch piece ginger, thinly sliced
- 1 tablespoon fish sauce
- 1 tablespoon sugar
- Salt, to taste

For the soup:

- 200g dried vermicelli noodles
- 200g cooked chicken breast, thinly sliced
- 2 eggs
- 2 tablespoons vegetable oil
- 2 shallots, thinly sliced
- 1/2 cup dried shrimp, soaked in water for 10 minutes and drained
- 1/2 cup shiitake mushrooms, thinly sliced
- 1/2 cup green onions, thinly sliced
- 1/2 cup cilantro leaves, chopped
- 1/4 cup Vietnamese mint leaves (optional)
- Ground black pepper, to taste

For garnish:

- Fried shallots
- Fresh cilantro leaves
- Lime wedges
- Sliced chili (optional)

Instructions:

1. Prepare the Broth:

- In a large pot, combine chicken broth, halved onion, thinly sliced ginger, fish sauce, sugar, and salt. Bring the mixture to a boil over high heat.
    - Reduce the heat to low and let the broth simmer gently for about 30 minutes to allow the flavors to meld. Strain the broth and discard the solids. Keep the broth warm over low heat.
2. Cook the Vermicelli Noodles:
    - Cook the dried vermicelli noodles in a separate pot of boiling water according to the package instructions until they are al dente. Drain and set aside.
3. Prepare the Soup Ingredients:
    - In a small bowl, beat the eggs. Heat vegetable oil in a non-stick skillet over medium heat. Pour the beaten eggs into the skillet and swirl to create a thin omelette. Cook for about 1-2 minutes until set. Remove the omelette from the skillet and let it cool slightly. Roll it up and slice it thinly into strips.
    - In the same skillet, sauté the thinly sliced shallots until golden brown and crispy. Remove from the skillet and set aside.
    - In the same skillet, add soaked dried shrimp and sliced shiitake mushrooms. Sauté for a few minutes until the mushrooms are tender and the shrimp are cooked through.
4. Assemble the Soup:
    - Divide the cooked vermicelli noodles among serving bowls. Top with cooked chicken breast slices, sliced omelette strips, sautéed dried shrimp and mushrooms, and sliced green onions.
    - Ladle the hot broth over the ingredients in each bowl.
5. Garnish and Serve:
    - Garnish each bowl with chopped cilantro leaves, Vietnamese mint leaves (if using), fried shallots, and ground black pepper.
    - Serve the Vietnamese Bun Thang Soup with Chicken, Egg, and Vermicelli hot with lime wedges and sliced chili on the side, if desired.

Enjoy your delicious homemade Vietnamese Bun Thang Soup with Chicken, Egg, and Vermicelli! It's a light and nourishing dish that's bursting with flavor.

Korean Kimchi Jjigae Soup with Pork Belly and Tofu

Ingredients:

- 2 cups kimchi, chopped
- 200g pork belly, thinly sliced
- 1 block (about 300g) firm tofu, cut into cubes
- 4 cups water or unsalted chicken broth
- 2 green onions, chopped
- 2 cloves garlic, minced
- 1 tablespoon gochugaru (Korean red pepper flakes)
- 1 tablespoon gochujang (Korean red pepper paste)
- 1 tablespoon soy sauce
- 1 tablespoon sesame oil
- 1 tablespoon vegetable oil
- Salt, to taste

Optional ingredients:

- 1 small onion, sliced
- 1/2 cup sliced mushrooms (such as shiitake or button mushrooms)
- 1 teaspoon fish sauce
- 1 teaspoon sugar

Instructions:

1. Prepare the Ingredients:
    - Heat vegetable oil in a large pot over medium heat. Add minced garlic and chopped green onions. Sauté for a minute until fragrant.
    - Add thinly sliced pork belly to the pot. Cook until the pork is browned and cooked through.
2. Add Kimchi and Seasonings:
    - Add chopped kimchi to the pot. Stir-fry for a few minutes until the kimchi is slightly softened and aromatic.
    - Stir in gochugaru (Korean red pepper flakes) and gochujang (Korean red pepper paste) until well combined.
3. Add Water/Broth and Bring to a Boil:
    - Pour water or unsalted chicken broth into the pot. Bring the mixture to a boil over medium-high heat.
4. Simmer and Add Tofu:

        - Once boiling, reduce the heat to medium-low and let the soup simmer for about 15-20 minutes, allowing the flavors to meld.
        - Add the cubed tofu to the pot. Simmer for another 5 minutes.
5. Season and Serve:
        - Stir in soy sauce and sesame oil. Taste the soup and adjust the seasoning with salt, sugar, and fish sauce if needed.
        - Serve the Korean Kimchi Jjigae Soup hot, garnished with additional chopped green onions, if desired.

Enjoy your delicious homemade Korean Kimchi Jjigae Soup with Pork Belly and Tofu! It's a comforting and spicy dish that pairs perfectly with a bowl of steamed rice.